An ABC of English Teaching

By the same author

NEW ENGLISH
a complete secondary English course

New English First
New English Second
New English Third
New English Fourth (to CSE)
A New English Course (to 'O' level)

Poetry Anthologies edited by Rhodri Jones

Themes Series

Men and Beasts
Imagination
Conflict
Generations
Men at Work
Town and Country

Preludes Series

Families
Work and Play
Weathers
Five Senses

Heinemann Short Stories* edited by Rhodri Jones

Book One—My World
Book Two—Other Worlds, Other Places
Book Three—Facing Up to the World
Book Four—The World Around Us
Book Five—The World Ahead

*forthcoming

An ABC of English Teaching

RHODRI JONES

Headmaster, John Kelly Boys' High School, Brent

HEINEMANN EDUCATIONAL BOOKS

LONDON

Heinemann Educational Books
22 Bedford Square London WC1B 3HH

LONDON EDINBURGH MELBOURNE AUCKLAND
HONG KONG SINGAPORE KUALA LUMPUR
NEW DELHI IBADAN NAIROBI JOHANNESBURG
EXETER (NH) KINGSTON PORT OF SPAIN

British Library C.I.P. Data
Jones, Rhodri
  ABC of English teaching.
  1. English language—Study and teaching
  (Secondary)—Great Britain
  2. English literature—Study and teaching
  (Secondary)—Great Britain
  I. Title
  428   LB1631
  ISBN 0-435-10490-X

Printed in Great Britain by
Butler & Tanner Ltd, Frome and London

Contents

Introduction

This book is offered in the hope that it will be of use to teachers of English and to students preparing to teach English. It concentrates on the practicalities of English teaching in the classroom rather than on theories or research. Some of the entries may be controversial or may stimulate discussion or may suggest new methods of approach; many may cover ground that appears to be already well-known and familiar. Nevertheless, it is hoped that by gathering them together in one volume, they will present a full survey of what the teaching of English involves. The entries are arranged in alphabetical order for easy reference.

A secondary purpose of this book is to provide a guide to how the course *New English* can be used and to indicate where specific material on particular points can be found in *New English*. This information as well as booklists and suggestions of other material available is supplied at the end of each entry. Cross-references to other entries should help to ensure that all aspects of the subject are covered. After entries, **A** indicates references to *New English*; **B** suggests other books which could be useful; **C** refers the reader to other entries.

Abbreviations
Throughout the book, the pupils' books in the *New English* series are referred to as follows:
NE1 = *New English First*
NE2 = *New English Second*
NE3 = *New English Third*
NE4 = *New English Fourth*
NEC = *A New English Course*

Activities

English lessons can too often become very static affairs with the teacher at the front and pupils sitting firmly ensconced in their desks. Anyone who has sat in on someone else's lesson knows how hard the classroom seats can become and how boring it can be simply to sit there as a passive observer—no matter how interesting or stimulating the teacher may be. If you haven't had this experience recently, try it, and you will gain some appreciation of what pupils have to put up with day in and day out.

Clearly, sitting still at a desk is often necessary with much of the work of the English lesson, but any opportunity for introducing movement or allowing some variation in this routine should be grasped—provided over-all control can still be retained. Drama is an obvious example. Filming and recording are other cases. Here are some less obvious activities which could provide variety or an opportunity for some of the pupils legitimately to get out of their seats.

Group discussion or group writing is one way of giving pupils a chance to reorganize the furniture and allowing them to exchange ideas with different sections of the class. For formal debates or general discussions, the classroom could be arranged so that pupils sit in a circle. The same could be done if a pupil is giving a talk or reporting back on a piece of research or if there is a visitor (a policeman talking about his work or an official talking about the RSPCA or Help the Aged).

Pupils doing research on a particular topic or interviewing other pupils about their views would allow for some movement within the class. Research or finding poems or other material on a subject would ideally be done in the library, but it may have to be done in the classroom, possibly with a number of pupils using a particular reference book and switching groups as required. The finding of display material (perhaps from magazines) and the arranging of this material on the wall would provide some pupils with the chance to get out of their seats.

Where possible, get the children out of the classroom completely—on an expedition to take photographs or to look at local shops and traffic or to do a survey of shops and housing in the area or simply on visits to places of interest and relevance to the theme being studied (it may be the zoo, the law courts, a local factory, a farm). Visits like these require careful planning and organization. There needs to be preliminary briefing. Specific points for pupils to look out for need to be stressed. There should perhaps even be worksheets for the pupils to fill in, as there is a danger that such visits could be formless and unmotivated. Nevertheless, the trouble is usually worthwhile, as a move outside the classroom is a welcome break in the routine, and pupils come back with a supply of fresh information and experience which will feed subsequent work.

A.   Each unit in *New English* has an Activities section with suggestions for drama and other activities of the kind outlined in this entry.

C.   See also DEBATES, DISPLAY, DRAMA, FILMS, GROUP WORK, LIBRARY, RESEARCH, SPEECHES, SURVEYS, TAPE RECORDING, VISITS.

Advanced Level

The first thing to make sure of is that students who are interested in studying for the Advanced Level of the General Certificate of Education are aware that this is an examination in English Literature and not English Language. There have been rumblings suggesting that there ought to be an 'A' Level in English Language, and this would be a very interesting and useful examination, but as yet only English Literature is examined at Advanced Level. Anyone attracted by the idea of 'A' Level in English must start therefore with one very important characteristic: he must enjoy reading. If he doesn't, then he is going to find the course boring and effortful. It would also help if he enjoys writing about what he has read and has a natural sympathy for what he reads and the intellectual curiosity to probe into the author's mind and motives. But that may be asking too much.

It is difficult to generalize about the various syllabuses offered by examining boards as they differ greatly and there is considerable choice. Students usually have to study some Chaucer and some Shakespeare, but they may then choose works from different periods, concentrate on one particular period (such as the Romantic Age or the Modern Age) or on a particular genre (such as satire). When choosing a suitable syllabus, it should be borne in mind that only a small minority of students taking 'A' Level English will go on to university to study English as a main subject, and the criterion should therefore be what is likely to appeal most to the average student. This will probably be the syllabus which puts the emphasis on modern literature as this is closest in feeling and language to the student. Eighteenth-century literature, for instance, is in language, style and attitude very remote from the experience of most young people today who do not have a special feeling for English literature or intend to study the subject at university.

Since syllabuses and texts differ so much, only generalized advice can be given here. One vexed question concerns the whole approach to 'A' Level. Should you concentrate from the very beginning on the prescribed texts, or should you spend a term or the whole of the first year on building up general literary background? It takes courage to choose the latter course, but it will probably pay off in providing the student with a greater knowledge and deeper critical sense from which he can embark on the prescribed texts and get to grips with them with a more mature understanding. This approach also enables the teacher to choose texts in the first instance which are more likely to interest the student and which are of a more appropriate level for his degree of understanding. The teacher will have to be strong enough too to ward off cries of 'What has this to do with the examination?'

The ability to write essays—to organize ideas, to marshal evidence and evince a knowledge of the texts—is a prerequisite of success in the 'A' Level English examination, as it is with other subjects. Yet surprisingly little time is spent on training students on how to do this. Too often, they are expected to come to the task fully fledged. There is a tremendous gap between the kind of recounting of facts expected and accepted at 'O' Level and the kind of sustained thought and logical progression of argument that is required for a good pass at 'A' Level. It may be necessary to work out paragraph plans and to present specimen essays in order to show students how it should be done. Time spent on collecting evidence for an essay—the kind of points to make, the kind of quotations to select—and on organizing the step-by-step development of this material into a convincing argument is time valuably spent. The need to make sure that students actually answer the question being asked cannot be overstressed.

The unseen comprehension and appreciation question is a common factor of most 'A' Level examination papers. It is here that spending a large part of the first year on extending general literary experience by reading and studying novels, plays, and poems of more immediate interest to the students pays off. They can come to the comprehension exercise and the poem they are expected to comment on with a greater width of literary knowledge. If students concentrate on the prescribed texts, then a separate course in evaluating prose and verse passages devised by the teacher or taken from an appropriate textbook will have to be resorted to.

Discussion is the essence of 'A' Level studies. It is not the place for the teacher to dictate notes and expect his students to reproduce them—though it may come to this if he is unfortunate enough to have students incapable of thinking for themselves. Ideally, this should be an opportunity for ideas about life as well as literature to be generated, and much depends on the enthusiasm and vitality of the teacher to be able to spark off a response in his students— even to shock or antagonize them into some kind of action or re-action. If the 'A' Level class is not a 'talking shop', then it is failing in its purpose, as it is only through this kind of give and take that the student can be encouraged to think for himself and to grow in his critical awareness.

A possibility is to conduct a seminar system whereby students read out their essays for consideration and criticism from the rest of the group including the teacher. This could be extended to include situa-tions where students take over responsibility for initiating discussion of a particular aspect of a text—for instance, the structure, an analysis of a character, aspects of style, thematic development, the signifi-cance of a particular episode. This gives the student the valuable experience of having to present his views clearly in public and having to defend them in the face of criticism. It also provides the oppor-tunity of covering a great deal of ground in a very economical space of time.

When we come to Chaucer or Shakespeare or even some seven-teenth or eighteenth-century texts, we come up against the problem of language. It is probably necessary to spend a lot of time crawling through the text to make sure that students really understand what the language means. With Chaucer, this may be obvious, but even with later texts it is too easy to assume that students understand what the words mean: they don't, and much slow painstaking study has to be undertaken to ensure that a basic level of understanding has been achieved before the more interesting work of interpretation can begin. This is another area where students can be given individual assignments of explaining particular sections of the text to the others, thus sharing out the work-load.

Background work on a writer like Chaucer can also be undertaken and should provide the student with a clearer idea of the context in which the author wrote. Areas such as the following could be examined: the London of Chaucer's day, the Peasants' Revolt, reli-gious dissent, the court, the universities and schools, *Piers Plowman*, contemporary medical beliefs, rhetoric, astrology. The General Prologue to *The Canterbury Tales* and tales appertaining to 'the marriage debate' should also be studied, even if only in the trans-lations by David Wright or Nevill Coghill. Lectures on the art, archi-tecture, and history of the period can be given by colleagues, and

4

if there is a cathedral or medieval coaching inn handy it should be visited. By building up background information in this way, the student can come to the text with a greater appreciation and understanding.

The same kind of inter-disciplinary approach can be applied to Shakespeare and other major figures of English literature. It can too easily be taken for granted that students have a wide awareness of the cultural and historical backgrounds of the texts that they are studying: this is not necessarily so.

Background reading too is important and should be encouraged. If a novel by Jane Austen is a prescribed text, read two more by the same author. If *Antony and Cleopatra* is on the list, read another tragedy by Shakespeare and another Roman play. In the sphere of drama, this can sometimes be made easier by going to see parallel Shakespeare plays in the theatre, and of course every effort should be made to see a prescribed play itself in the theatre—or on film as a second best. A workshop production of the play by the group, where this can be organized, can tremendously enlarge the understanding of the play—even if it leads only to a greater awareness of what actually happens in the play.

When it comes to critical background reading, the situation is more difficult. The critical writing available tends to be either too simple, like the 'O' Level English Literature notes on texts, or too abstruse for sixth formers, like the works of William Empson, Cleanth Brooks and F. R. Leavis, which are really designed for university specialists. Care has to be taken in the kind of critical work recommended for general consumption. Here are some 'middle range' books that would be worth exploring:

The Arden Shakespeare (Methuen)
Preface Books (Longman)
Studies in English Literature (Arnold)
The Casebook Series (Macmillan)
Twentieth Century Views (Prentice Hall)
Profiles in Literature (Routledge and Kegan Paul)
The Critical Idiom (Methuen)
Stratford-upon-Avon Studies (Arnold)
Literature in Perspective (Evans)
Study-Guide Series (Macmillan)
Writers and Critics (Oliver and Boyd)
Authors in their Age (Blackie)

Since a student studying 'A' Level English Literature spends so much time reading and criticizing literature, it has always seemed strange that he is not expected to write any himself. There are some peripheral attempts to introduce creative writing or course work to 'A' Level studies, but these have not yet gained much ground. As an aid to 'A' Level studies, however, encouraging students to produce some imaginative work of their own is very valuable and can help them to gain an insight into what literature is about and how an author's mind works. The study of imagery, for instance, could lead to students being expected to write a poem. They could be asked to write a short story using a situation similar to one in their texts. If appropriate, they could be asked to write a sonnet—it may not be a very good sonnet, but at least they will have the experience of struggling with the mechanics of the form and may appreciate better the skill of the poet. Voluntary creative writing of their own should also be encouraged and sympathetically discussed.

Another approach that could be explored is the writing of parodies and imitations. In this way, creative writing and critical understanding are combined. The standard authors—Chaucer, Spenser, Shakespeare, Milton, Wordsworth, Keats, Browning, Eliot—lend themselves very much to this kind of approach. In order to write good parodies or imitations, the students have to have some understanding of the particular characteristics and pre-occupations of the poet, and the success or otherwise of the parody or imitation says a great deal about a student's genuine appreciation.

If possible, the teacher should try to create an interest in contemporary literature and contemporary arts so that prescribed texts are not seen in isolation but as part of a literary process that is still continuing. Visits to the theatre and cinema, for instance, are important. Plays are essentially not to be studied but to be seen. Every effort should be made to see in the theatre or at least on film any play being discussed, as well as other plays and films of interest. The reading of novels other than prescribed texts should be encouraged through the school bookshop, the local library, or by having a sixth-form paperback library which is constantly being added to. Reviews of new novels and newspaper interviews with writers should be pinned up. Literary magazines (such as *Stand*, *London Magazine*, *New Review*, *The Critical Quarterly*) should be readily available and students should be specifically referred to them. An interest in poetry can be stimulated by the visit of a real poet to read and discuss his work through the Arts Council's 'Writers in Schools' scheme. There may be an Arts Society in your area which organizes exhibitions, talks and other events; if so, arrange for students to be informed of it and to visit it. The sixth form could organize its own literary and dramatic society to invite speakers, show films, arrange visits, and put on debates and readings. In these ways, it may be possible for students to become aware that literature in particular and the arts in general belong to a live tradition and are not simply objects for academic study in order to achieve an examination pass.

A.   *New English* is designed to lead pupils to GCE 'O' Level English Language or CSE, but a close study of the many literary extracts included should prove a good foundation for the kind of enquiring approach necessary for 'A' Level.

B.   'A' Level English syllabuses vary so much that it is not possible to provide a composite list of recommended critical books. For the comprehension and appreciation paper, the following are worth considering:

Literature and Criticism, H. Coombs (Penguin)
Reading and Response, R. P. Hewett (Harrap)
Understanding Literature, Robin Mayhead (CUP)
The Practice of Criticism, D. H. Rawlinson (CUP)
The Appreciation of Poetry, P. Gurrey (OUP)
The Practical Criticism of Poetry, C. B. Cox and A. E. Dyson (Arnold)
Modern Poetry, C. B. Cox and A. E. Dyson (Arnold)
An Introduction to English Poetry, Lawrence Lerner (Arnold)
An Introduction to Literary Criticism, S. M. Schreiber (Wheaton)
The Critical Examination, Malcolm C. Peet and David Robinson (Wheaton)
Take Two, Alan Bolt (Harrap)

Advertisements

Advertisements play an important part in everyone's life, and all of us are influenced by them to some extent—even if we like to think they have no power over us. (This could be one topic for class discussion—Are people affected by advertisements? Have you any evidence for this? Can you think of any specific instances? Why do firms spend so much money on advertising if it has no effect?) Advertisements also manipulate language in a particular way, and it is important to alert our pupils to this fact so that they can analyse it and be aware of it and perhaps be protected from it. There is also a great deal of readily available material about advertisements— namely, the advertisements themselves to be found in newspapers and magazines—which can be used in the classroom.

The following questions about advertising need to be discussed and can form the basis for a lesson on the subject:

Why do people advertise?

How effective is advertising?

What makes a good advertisement?

What kinds of emotions does advertising appeal to? (e.g. greed, envy, humour, nostalgia, sex, fear, snobbery). Give examples.

Is advertising fair or moral?

Does advertising create dissatisfaction?

Another approach is to ask pupils to find examples of advertisements to bring into the classroom to comment on and discuss—or else the teacher can provide a supply. (The Sunday colour supplements provide a fruitful source.) Individual advertisements can be analysed—What is the thinking behind them? What are they appealing to? What is the relation between word and image, and which is more important? Why are they effective or ineffective? Pupils could be asked to specialize in particular areas. Cars, soap, drink, cigarettes, food are subjects where material abounds.

Advertising on television deserves a lesson to itself. Find out what the favourite advertisements are and why. If possible, record the words, music, and sounds of some advertisements so that they can be considered in isolation from the visual image. At the same time, the expertise with which many television advertisements are made could be analysed—the cutting, the choice of locations, the number of actors involved, the well-known actors who appear, the use of famous 'voice overs', the slickness of what passes in front of the eyes in a fifteen second slot, the use of atmospheric music. A special study could be undertaken of television advertisements that appeal to nostalgia or sophistication or our sense of humour.

The language of advertisements is important, whether it appears in print or is heard on television or on commercial radio. Words like exclusive, only, special, new, original, unique, improved, take on a particular meaning. Pupils or teacher could find examples to discuss. Advertisements for the armed forces or the police are often very revealing in the kind of language they use and are worth duplicating for class discussion.

Advertisements on hoardings have to make a strong and immediate impact on passers-by or on motorists, so what do they concentrate on? A discussion of some currently on view could be productive.

Small ads in newspapers are also worth looking at. Cost is an important element here—how to give all the relevant details in as few words as possible. Pupils could be asked to write their own small ads as economically as possible for items they want to sell or buy.

The same applies to advertisements in general: pupils should be given the opportunity of making their own advertisements, inventing the names of their products, and using a mixture of words and pictures (their own drawings or collages of pictorial material cut from magazines). This can be done either in the English lesson or in collaboration with the art department.

Advertising jingles can also produce a profitable area for discussion and imagination. Find out what the current jingles are, ask why advertisers use jingles, and then encourage pupils to write their own.

If possible, invite a speaker to talk about advertising. It could be someone working in journalism or television or from an advertising agency. Actually having someone in the classroom whose life is involved in advertising can provide lively personal experience to counter the danger of discussing the subject in a vacuum and in the abstract.

A.   Unit 4 of NE4 is devoted to the world of advertising. Material for developing the ideas in this entry will be found there.

B.   The following books could provide useful additional ideas and material:
The Hidden Persuaders, Vance Packard (Penguin)
The Question of Advertising, Michael Marland (Hart Davis)
Break for Commercials, Edith Rudinger and Vic Kelly (Penguin)
Discrimination and Popular Culture, ed. Denys Thompson (Penguin)
The Persuaders, R. B. Heath (Nelson)
Resources for Learning, L. C. Taylor (Penguin)
Nine Themes for English Teachers, Cary Bagalgette and David Pepper (published privately; available from the Local Centre for English, Holloway School, Hilldrop Road, London N.7).

Aims of English Teaching

We tend to assume that we know what we are doing when we teach English. But it is useful to sit down as an individual or as a department to think about what exactly our aims are. One clear aim is the necessity to provide our pupils with the basic skills of communication—reading, writing, and oracy. We need to equip them so that they can cope socially—so that they can read and fill in forms, so that they can talk coherently on the telephone or present their case when stopped by the police, so that they can distinguish between fact and fiction or partial views as expressed in newspapers and advertisements.

Another aim may be to give our pupils an awareness of the range and variety of English literature; to show them what has been achieved in the past and to provide them with an aesthetic experience so that they can appreciate great literature when they encounter it. They should know about and admire Shakespeare and Dickens, Jane Austen and George Eliot, Tennyson and Browning. The trouble here is that if we are talking about pupils of all abilities there is bound to be a problem of understanding. The authors named were writing for an adult audience. To what extent is it reasonable to expect young people to be able to understand and appreciate them?

A third aim is contained in the idea of 'personal growth'. English is a subject where pupils can explore experience and sort out their own ideas and gain maturity through reading and writing and talking. Many people see this as the most important aspect of English, providing the opportunity for pupils to think deeply about themselves and the world around them and therefore providing the chance for them to grow as people.

A fourth aim which deserves consideration is the need to provide pupils with some kind of paper qualification in English to show to a future employer that they have reached a particular standard. Some teachers may feel that regular examination practice is essential if pupils are to get the kind of results that they deserve or require, and that to ignore this fact of life is, in a way, letting the pupils down.

It is possible that all four aims are equally valid and equally important. Alternatively, some may feel that one is more important than the others. What matters is that English teachers should think about what they are supposed to be doing and be clear in their own minds what their priorities are. This might be a useful basis for discussion at a departmental meeting.

A. *New English* tries to hold a balance of these four aims, though perhaps the 'heritage of English literature' view is least strongly represented.

B. The following books provide a much fuller discussion of some of the points raised here:
Growth Through English, John Dixon (OUP)
English in Practice, eds. Geoffrey Summerfield and Stephen Tunnicliffe (CUP)
The Disappearing Dais, Frank Whitehead (Hart Davis)
English Teaching, Albert Rowe (Hart Davis)
Every English Teacher, Anthony Adams and John Pearce (OUP)

English for Maturity, David Holbrooke (CUP)
Directions in the Teaching of English, ed. Denys Thompson (CUP)
English for Diversity, Peter Abbs (Heinemann)
Teaching English, John Walsh (Heinemann)
The Intelligence of Feeling, Robert Witkin (Heinemann)
The Humanities Jungle, Antony Adams (Ward Lock)
Matters of interest and importance to English teachers are discussed in the following quarterly journals:
The Use of English (Hart Davis)
English in Education (published by the National Association for the Teaching of English)
Teaching London Kids (published by the London association for the Teaching of English)

C. See also DEPARTMENTAL MEETINGS, EXAMINATIONS, SKILLS, SYLLABUS.

Anthologies

Anthologies of verse or prose, or a mixture of the two, can provide valuable teaching material. Even where an English department has worked out its own course and duplicated its own material, sets of anthologies can be useful in providing the necessary poem or extract to use with a class. By their very nature, anthologies are meant to be dipped into rather than to be slavishly followed page by page. Any given anthology will contain items a particular teacher will not wish to use, and the same poem or extract can appear in a number of different anthologies. Fortunately, the converse is also true, and any good anthology ought to contain a large amount of material the teacher will want to use and items which cannot readily be found anywhere else.

Once, anthologies consisted solely of the printed word. Now, they tend to contain a great deal of illustrative matter, partly to make the books more attractive to pupils and to disguise the fact that they are textbooks, and partly to provide visual stimulus related to the words and complementing the words. But when some recent anthologies divide the pages more or less equally between words and pictures, it may be time to question whether this trend hasn't perhaps gone too far.

Another point worth considering is whether anthologies should be resources or teaching texts; whether the book should consist simply of a collection of poems or prose extracts or whether there should also be suggestions on how to use this material, with comprehension questions directed at the pupil and indications of follow-up work that can be done. The answer is probably both.

Ideally, every teacher should build up his own personal anthology of pieces of writing which he has used and which he knows, from experience, work. There are times when pupils also should be encouraged to make collections of poems, for instance, on a particular theme. These can be gathered together in booklets which could perhaps be used as reading books or as resources for work with another class.

A. Each unit in *New English* contains a number of prose extracts and poems about a particular theme which could be regarded as a mini-anthology. The Reading Lists also direct attention to other sources that could be used to provide further material. The Activities sections often suggest opportunities for pupils to make their own anthologies—for instance, a collection of pictures and poems about Christmas in Unit 4 of NE1; a collection of poems about the sea in Unit 2 of NE2; a class anthology of poems describing animals hunting or being hunted in Unit 5 of NE3; a collection of poems about war in NE4, Unit 8.

B. The following anthologies indicate something of the range available and are worth exploring. First of all poetry anthologies:
Tunes on a Tin Whistle, ed. Alan Crang (Wheaton)
Dragonsteeth, ed. Eric Williams (Arnold)
Rising Early, ed. Charles Causley (Longman)
Please Yourself, ed. Ann Owen (Longman)
Happenings, eds. Maurice Wollman and David Grudgeon (Harrap)
A Choice of Poets, ed. R. P. Hewett (Harrap)
Seven Themes in Modern Verse, ed. Maurice Wollman (Harrap)
Themes, ed. Rhodri Jones (Heinemann)
Preludes, ed. Rhodri Jones (Heinemann)
Iron, Honey, Gold, ed. David Holbrook (CUP)
Wordscapes, ed. Barry Maybury (OUP)
Thoughtshapes, ed. Barry Maybury (OUP)
Every Man Will Shout, eds. Roger Mansfield and Isobel Armstrong (OUP)
Voices, ed. Geoffrey Summerfield (Penguin)
Junior Voices, ed. Geoffrey Summerfield (Penguin)
Touchstones, eds. M. G. and P. Benton (EUP)
The following anthologies or series provide prose and verse:
Oxford English Source Books, Nancy Martin (OUP)
Reflections, Simon Clements, John Dixon and Leslie Stratta (OUP)

The English Project (Ward Lock)
Impact, R. H. Poole and P. J. Shepherd (Heinemann)
Junior Impact, R. H. Poole and P. J. Shepherd (Heinemann)
Readings, Richard Doubleday (Heinemann)
Insight, Alan Cattell and Alexandra Penniall (Harrap)
The Explorations Series (Wheaton)
Dimensions (Wheaton)

One development which allows the teacher more easily to use those parts of an anthology which he finds useful is the publication of material in the form of work sheets or poetry cards, or material which is published in separate units. See, for instance:
English Broadsheets, Peter Abbs (Heinemann)
Leopards, eds. Denys Thompson and Christopher Parry (CUP)
Poetry Pack, ed. James Gibson and Raymond Wilson (Macmillan)
Poetrycards, eds. C. Copeman and D. Self (Macmillan)

C. See also ACTIVITIES, COURSE BOOKS, POETRY, READING LISTS, SPOUT, TEN ESSENTIAL POEMS, THEMES.

Assessment

Some definite procedure is essential to check that pupils are making progress and that pupils with particular problems are not overlooked. Normally, this will depend on the efficiency and vigilance of the class teacher. Whenever he has a new class to teach, he should be on the look-out for signs that may give cause for concern, and certainly within the first month he should have noted pupils who are left-handed, slow writers, slow readers, and poor spellers. Consultation with the remedial department will probably be necessary so that pupils with particular problems can be referred there for special help. It would be useful to have a meeting of members of the English department about a month after the beginning of the autumn term where specific cases can be discussed.

There may be differences of opinion about whether tests or examinations are required at the end of each term or each year. Where testing to gauge specific reading or learning problems is concerned, this is probably best left to the remedial department. Testing or examining to measure general progress is probably unnecessary: a conscientious teacher should be able to tell from his contact with the pupil and by means of continuous assessment whether the pupil's writing and understanding of reading are increasing in maturity and skill. Formal examinations become relevant only if a year group is going to be divided into sets or if a decision has to be made about whether a pupil should be entered for 'O' level or CSE.

The public examinations in the fifth year can provide an assessment of whether a pupil would benefit from going on to an 'A' Level course. But examination results can be misleading and the teacher's knowledge of his pupil's ability ought to be much wider and more perceptive. Each case should be considered on its individual merits and both the examination result and the teacher's personal knowledge taken into account.

A. The Consolidation sections which appear periodically throughout *New English* may be used to test that pupils have mastered the specific points raised in previous units, but the results should not be taken as indications of literary skill or innate ability. Unit 11 of NE4 contains specimen examination papers suitable for CSE and 'O' Level which could be used as tests to decide which pupils should prepare for and sit which examination.

C. See also CORRECTION OF WORK, EXAMINATIONS, REMEDIAL ENGLISH.

Audiences

It is very easy for some of the activities of the English lesson—especially writing—to become artificial and to take place in a vacuum. This is to some extent inevitable because of the very nature of the teaching–learning process, but some attempts can be made to reduce this artificiality. One way is to ensure a variety of 'audiences' towards which pupils direct their writing, discussion, drama, and research and thus try to create a purposefulness and an objective which might otherwise be lacking.

The teacher himself is an obvious audience, and since this is so, it determines the kind of relationship that must exist between class and teacher. It must be such that the pupil feels confident that he can speak and write freely and wants to communicate. In this connection, the teacher's response is vital; criticism must be tempered with sympathy, and there must be a genuine interest in what the pupil is communicating if the pupil's confidence is to be maintained.

Directing talk and writing towards other pupils provides another realistic audience. For instance, there is more point in research if the findings are then going to be passed on to the rest of the class, or in writing a story if it is going to be displayed on the wall or in a class or school magazine for other pupils to read.

Real audiences outside the classroom are more difficult to find.

One possibility is the writing of letters to organizations asking for information or requesting material, or inviting speakers to come to the school and thanking them for giving up their time, or making arrangements to visit places of interest.

It is surprising how many people *will* be glad to come and talk about their work or their life. For pupils, this can form an excellent introduction to public speaking and to the formal etiquette required. Care has to be taken over inviting politicians, but organizers of voluntary bodies such as youth centres, Rotarians, Samaritans and charitable organizations are often pleased to be invited.

Another way of providing a real audience is to encourage pupils to take part in a literary competition. This can sometimes provide a stimulus. Local newspapers and firms often organize competitions which give an opportunity for pupils to write with a definite objective in view. The best known competition is the annual Children's Literary Competition, once organized by the *Daily Mirror* and now run by W. H. Smith (Ibis Information Services Ltd., Waterside, Lowbell Lane, London Colney, St Albans, Herts.). The best work is published by Heinemann Educational Books in the series of volumes entitled *Children as Writers* which make useful anthologies of accessible material for class use and can give pupils an idea of the kind of standard expected of them.

Imaginary audiences are more easy to create. There are letters to newspapers, replies to advertisements, letters to friends and relations, arguments presented to support or attack particular points of view, explanations for the benefit of a visitor from outer space.

One final audience that deserves consideration is the examiner who marks and grades the final examination paper. Pupils should be alerted to what his requirements are. He should be presented not as an ogre but as someone who is looking for fresh and interesting ideas and is only too delighted when he finds them. Writing for an examiner should be seen as an opportunity for the pupil to show what he can achieve.

C. See also ACTIVITIES, DEBATES, DISCUSSIONS, DRAMA, LETTERS, MAGAZINE, RESEARCH, SCHOOL PLAY, WRITING.

Books for Young Adults
See CLASS READERS, NOVELS.

Certificate of Secondary Education

CSE is designed to be a two-year course in the 4th and 5th years of the secondary school. This examination was set up to provide for the needs of the top 60 per cent of the ability range. It is not a pass/fail examination; there are five grades from 1 to 5 and an Unclassified section. Grade 1 is equivalent to a pass at GCE 'O' Level. Grade 4 is considered to represent average ability in the subject. There is much more teacher involvement in devising syllabuses, setting examinations and allocating grades. A CSE syllabus and examination can be set by the central examining board (Mode I); by a consortium of schools which get together to devise their course and examination (Mode II); by an individual school (Mode III). By using Mode II or Mode III examinations, it is possible therefore to tailor the course to the particular requirements of your own school or area.

There are normally three elements in a CSE syllabus and examination: course work, oral examination, and written examination. Course work is a selection of the writing done by the pupil during the two years of the course. It should include a variety of different kinds of writing—imaginative, personal, factual, critical, argumentative. A grade is awarded to this writing, and it counts towards the final result. The oral examination usually takes the form of a discussion group, and grades are allocated according to the skill and fluency of individual members of the group in talking about a chosen subject. The written examination consists of comprehension exercises, critical writing, and imaginative or factual writing.

CSE differs from GCE 'O' Level in that not everything depends on the final examination. Quite a considerable account is taken of the work the pupil does in the two years leading up to the examination. In CSE, one grade is awarded for work in English language and literature; in GCE, there are separate examinations and pupils can gain two separate passes in English language and English literature.

The approach to CSE is also different from that GCE. It can be freer and much more creative. The emphasis is on stimulating the imagination and reading for enjoyment. Discussion is an essential element. A pupil who gains a Grade 1 not only has some ability in and appreciation of the subject, but he has also worked for it. A Grade 1 folder of course work will contain really outstanding creative writing, something for which there is no equivalent at GCE.

The approach to GCE is more academic. It requires a greater degree of technical correctness in writing and a greater analytical skill in reading. In theory (and in practice) someone with a natural ability and intelligence could gain a pass at 'O' Level simply by doing well in the examination and without doing any preparation for it at all. This is something which always strikes me as rather unfair. Someone who gains a Grade 1 at CSE has really earned it.

Deciding whether a pupil should sit CSE or GCE can be difficult. The factors involved are technical accuracy, analytical skill in comprehension, skill and fluency in discussion, and imaginative ability. The first two are necessary for GCE; the latter two for CSE. It is possible for a pupil to pass GCE if he writes dully but accurately and if he is unable to put two words together in speech. In fact, it would be advisable to enter this kind of pupil for GCE. A pupil who can express his opinions volubly and who shows imagination in his writing, although things like spelling and sentence structure may be weak, would stand a better chance if entered for CSE.

When a decision is made about the examination a pupil will be taking varies from school to school. In some it is made at the beginning of the 4th year with CSE and GCE groups following separate two-year courses; in others the decision is left as late as possible with all pupils following a common course, usually based on CSE. The latter seems preferable. It allows for late development and ensures that potential GCE candidates are not restricted to a too narrow academic course.

Another factor which may sometimes influence decisions about entering a pupil for CSE or GCE is the attitude of outside agencies towards these examinations. Although most important institutions and industries accept that Grade 1 CSE is equivalent to a GCE pass, there is still a feeling among many parents and pupils that it is inferior. They feel that it will not be recognized and that it is better to be entered for 'O' Level and fail than to get a Grade 1 CSE. Persuasion and propaganda are necessary to overcome this prejudice.

There are plans to merge CSE and GCE and to have a common examination at 16+. This seems more feasible in English than in some other subjects and would eliminate the necessity of making difficult decisions about which examination a pupil should sit. The syllabus for such an examination would almost certainly be on the lines of CSE which could well be an advantage.

A. The first three volumes of *New English* are designed as a general course suitable for mixed ability groups and providing a basis for pupils taking either CSE or GCE. The final volume, NE4, provides a two-year course primarily for CSE candidates, but also for GCE candidates where it is felt they should not specialize too early. Pupils who sit GCE would obtain a sufficient grounding and general background from studying NE4. If it is felt that more specific training in 'O' Level is required, NEC by Rhodri Jones (Heine-mann) is available as an alternative text.

The Examination Practice sections of NE4 refer specifically to CSE.

C. See also AIMS OF ENGLISH TEACHING, COURSE WORK, EXAMINATIONS, ORDINARY LEVEL.

Children's Literature

The past twenty-five years have seen a remarkable development in the world of children's literature. There is now a large number of outstanding authors writing specially for young readers, and the general quality of the work being produced is very high. Of course, there have been good writers for children in the past, such as Mrs Molesworth, F. Hodgson Burnett, and E. Nesbit; there have also been authors who have now been, as it were, taken over by child-ren—authors such as Mark Twain, R. L. Stevenson, R. D. Black-more, Daniel Defoe, Charlotte Brontë, and, to some extent, Charles Dickens. But such authors are bound to have a certain remoteness for the average child today. The strong middle-class point of view and the literary or old-fashioned seeming language are likely to act as barriers to enjoyment and appreciation. Only children with a literary background could devour novels by these authors whole—though judiciously chosen extracts and a dramatic and enthusiastic reading by a teacher can still give most pupils a taste of them, and they can enrich and extend pupils' understanding.

Much less advocacy of this kind is necessary with modern writers for children and this is where their particular value lies. These authors write in the language of today and they write with children in mind. Their books provide the opportunity for young readers to identify with the characters and to share their experiences in a way that might not be possible with books written earlier. Pupils are more likely to be able to read complete novels and so gain extended literary experience.

And reading good children's novels does provide valuable literary experience. These writers deal with the same kind of themes and moral issues as the most serious of past or present writers for adults—at perhaps a less subtle and more approachable level, though the moral complexity is nevertheless considerable. A novel like Leon Garfield's *Smith*, for instance, as well as recounting the racy adventures of a twelve-year-old rascal of a pickpocket, also explores questions of justice, the search for truth, the difference between appearance and reality, the nature of heroism. Any pupil reading such a novel would not only enjoy the story but also emerge with a deeper awareness of the complexity of human life.

It is possible then for children's literature to provide material for an answer to the question which is the concern of writers for adults: How to live? It also provides a foundation on which pupils can base an appreciation of more mature literature. A pupil who has read Ivan Southall's *Hills End* in which a group of children have to struggle for survival on their own when floods threaten their homes will have a deeper understanding of the issues at stake when he later comes to read William Golding's *Lord of the Flies*.

The range and variety of children's novels available today is remarkable. There are the historical novels of Rosemary Sutcliff, Leon Garfield, and Hester Burton; the science fiction of Peter Dickinson, John Christopher, and André Norton; the family stories of Nina Bawden, Gillian Avery, and K. M. Peyton; the fantasy worlds created by Joan Aiken, Penelope Lively, and Alan Garner. And these are only a few of those writing with distinction for children today.

Obviously, not all children's writers appeal to all children, William Mayne is a case in point. His idiosyncratic style is not one that can necessarily be recommended to everyone. The whimsy of Joan Aiken and the Dickensian flamboyance of much of Leon Garfield may be acquired tastes. But there are many books by children's writers that can be used as class readers with all children and a vast range to appeal to every kind of individual. These are the books which pupils in the top junior classes and the first three years of the secondary school should be reading. These are the books which they will enjoy, which may encourage them in the reading habit, and which will lead them into a deeper appreciation of adult literature.

There are a number of series of edited classics available where the story is either retold in simplified language or in abbreviated form. In general, these are not successful. The value of a novel like *Vanity Fair* or *A Tale of Two Cities* lies not so much in its plot as in the richness of character, incident, and atmosphere, and this is lost when it is gutted to provide a simple and bare story-line. It is far better that pupils read novels especially written for them, with their own resonances and richnesses, than anaemic versions of the classics.

Every English teacher should try to keep abreast of current developments in children's literature and should read as many of the new novels which come out as he can so as to find further examples to use with his classes and so that he can make useful suggestions when advising individual pupils in their reading. Periodicals like *New Statesman*, *The Times Literary Supplement*, and *The Times Educational Supplement* have occasional special sections dealing with children's literature. *Books for your Children* (edited by Anne Wood) and *Growing Point* (edited by Margery Fisher) are specialist journals dealing with children's books. *Reviewsheet* (available from Jane Powell, Sydenham School, Dartmouth Road, London SE 26) gives detailed reviews of new fiction for young people and considers each book specifically from the point of view of its value or usefulness in the library or the classroom. The National Book League has an annual exhibition of the year's books and the annotated catalogue *Children's Books of the Year* (by Elaine Moss) is published by Hamish Hamilton. The quarterly journal of the School Library Association, *The School Librarian*, is also useful.

A. Extracts from authors mentioned in this entry can be found in *New English* as follows:

Gillian Avery, *A Likely Lad* (NE2, Unit 1)
Nina Bawden, *The Peppermint Pig* (NE1, Unit 8)
R. D. Blackmore, *Lorna Doone* (NE2, Unit 5)
Charlotte Brontë, *Jane Eyre* (NE1, Unit 2)
F. Hodgson Burnett, *The Secret Garden* (NE3, Unit 4)
John Christopher, *The White Mountains* (NE1, Unit 3)
Daniel Defoe, *Robinson Crusoe* (NE2, Unit 2)
Charles Dickens, *A Christmas Carol* (NE1, Unit 4)
    Oliver Twist (NE3, Unit 1)
    Great Expectations (NE3, Unit 6)
Alan Garner, *The Weirdstone of Brisingamen* (NE1, Unit 7)
William Golding, *Lord of the Flies* (NE3, Unit 2)
Penelope Lively, *The Ghost of Thomas Kempe* (NE2, Unit 4)
William Mayne, *The Fishing Party* (NE1, Unit 2)
    Plot Night (NE2, Unit 3)
K. M. Peyton, *Flambards* (NE3, Unit 5)
Ivan Southall, *Ash Road* (NE3, Unit 5)
    Josh (NE3, Unit 1)
R. L. Stevenson, *Kidnapped* (NE2, Unit 6)
Rosemary Sutcliff, *Dragonslayer* (NE1, Unit 3)
Mark Twain, *The Adventures of Huckleberry Finn* (NE1, Unit 1)
    The Adventures of Tom Sawyer (NE3, Unit 4)
    Autobiography (NE2, Unit 9)

Many further extracts from children's novels are used, particularly in the first three books, and many further titles are to be found in the Reading Lists which end each unit.

B. For further information about children's literature, see:
Choosing Books for Children, Peter Hollindale (Elek)
Intent upon Reading, Margery Fisher (Brockhampton)
A Sense of Story, John Rowe Townsend (Kestrel)
The Nesbit Tradition, The Children's Novel in England 1945–70,
    Marcus Crouch (Benn)
Children and Fiction, Wallace Hildick (Evans)
Written for Children, John Rowe Townsend (Kestrel)
Good Writers for Young Readers, ed. Denis Butts (Hart Davis)
How to Find out about Children's Literature, Alec Ellis (Wheaton)
Introducing Books to Children, Aidan Chambers (Heinemann)
Tales Out of School, Geoffrey Trease (Heinemann)
Reading Together, Kenyon Calthrop (Heinemann)
Children and their Books, Schools Council Research Studies (Mac-
    millan)
Only Connect, ed. Sheila Egoff (OUP)
Suitable for Children?, ed. Nicholas Tucker (Sussex University Press)
Writers, Critics and Children, ed. Geoffrey Fox (Heinemann)
The Cool Web: The Pattern of Children's Reading, ed. Margaret
    Meek, Aidan Warlow, and Griselda Barton (Bodley Head)
The Thorny Paradise, ed. Edward Blishen (Kestrel)

C. See also CLASS LIBRARIES, CLASS READERS, LIBRARY, NOVELS,
SILENT READING.

Class Libraries

To encourage reading, pupils can be issued with class readers for
silent reading or for reading at home. The trouble is that, without
the teacher's guidance or without careful selection, not all the pupils
in a class are necessarily going to find the same book interesting and
enjoyable. An alternative method is to allow pupils the run of the
library (perhaps during a library period) and require them to choose
their own reading material. The danger here is that pupils may be
overwhelmed by the choice available and may not be able to select
effectively. They may also be more attracted by books about football
or motor cars or witchcraft when what you want them to choose
are stories of quality that will entertain and extend.

    Probably the best solution is to have a class library available which
will allow for some selectivity but also for some individual choice.
This may, for reasons of accommodation, have to be a box of books
which is carried around, or, if you are lucky, a permanent bookcase

or cupboard. The choice of books available should be wide. There should be some non-fiction books (but not too many), some books specially written for the less able, some duplication of certain titles so that if one catches on there are further copies for interested pupils, and some demanding books which might well capture the imagination of particular individuals (*The Lord of the Rings* or *Watership Down* or Ursula le Guin's *The Earthsea Trilogy*, for example, for younger pupils; *Down and Out in Paris and London*, Richard Wright's *Black Boy* or Joseph Heller's *Catch-22* for older pupils). The teacher should be familiar with the books in the collection so that he can recommend particular books to pupils according to their tastes, needs, and abilities.

The establishment of a routine is a good thing with class libraries—a regular period each week when it is used, a proper procedure for returning and taking out books, an expected response to the books read (a five-line 'review'; compiling a list of reading; talking about the book to the rest of the class).

A. The Reading Lists in *New English* could provide some suitable titles with which to stock class libraries.

B. See the suggestions for further reading under the entries CHILDREN'S LITERATURE and CLASS READERS.

C. See also CHILDREN'S LITERATURE, CLASS READERS, LIBRARY, NOVELS, SILENT READING.

Class Readers

A class reader (that is, a particular book which the whole class reads) provides a shared experience with all pupils being treated as equal and with all pupils getting something out of the reading (though related to their ability). From this common experience can come work in which they can all join. It could be the discussion of points as they arise in the story—the revelation of character, the significance of particular actions, the explanation of words or ideas, the relating of one event or character to another. It could be written work which comes out of the reading and which is suggested by it. For instance, a class which has read William Golding's *Lord of the Flies* might go on to write a story of their own about a group of children marooned on a desert island and how they cope. The experience of reading the book will provide a background which will suggest some lines for development and against which they can measure their own imaginative efforts.

Class readers can be read in isolation as literary experiences valuable in themselves, but they are particularly useful when used as part of a theme. They act as a source of factual, emotional, and imaginative material related to the theme. For instance, if the theme being studied is the sea, the use of a class reader like Armstrong Sperry's *The Boy Who Was Afraid* or Theodore Taylor's *The Cay* would provide admirable back-up material. All sorts of ideas about the sea would arise from such a reading—the various moods of the sea, attitudes towards the sea, the vicarious experience of what it is like to live on the sea. But a class reader should not be studied solely for the light it casts on a particular theme. It should also be treated as a literary experience, and aspects of style, character, structure, and attitude should be discussed.

A class reader can be used as the basis of English teaching for a period of time with all the work being related to it or being derived from it. Sections of the book can be used as the basis for comprehension. Discussion can revolve around ideas raised by the book. Written work can be in the form of a response to the book, either by creating a similar situation (as in the example given from *Lord of the Flies*) or by descriptions of characters in the book or summaries of important episodes; other possibilities would be to write a further adventure involving the same characters or a continuation of the story.

There are different ways of organizing the reading of a class reader. It can be read by the teacher to the class; it can be read silently in class; it could be read at home; or there could be a combination of these various methods. With mixed ability classes, the first of these is probably the best as it ensures the maximum enjoyment and comprehension.

Class readers can be used successfully with mixed-ability classes. There are books which work well with all pupils with a reading age of 9+. Clearly, the choice of book is important, and the teacher must ensure not only that the language and ideas are within the grasp of his pupils, but also that it has an appeal to the particular age-group in mind. It is quite unrealistic, for example, to expect a mixed ability class to be able to cope with *The Mill on the Floss* or *Wuthering Heights* in totality as a class reader. An 'edited' version may be a possibility—either one of the rewritten editions or a reading of the main episodes connected by a summary of what happens in between supplied by the teacher—but see the views expressed under the entry CHILDREN'S LITERATURE.

Here is a selected list of books which have been successfully used as class readers with mixed ability classes. Note that the inclusion of a particular title for one age-group does not preclude its being used for another. Many of the books recommended for 1st-year classes could work equally well with top juniors or with 2nd-year classes. It depends on the particular class. The same is true of books recommended for the 4th- and 5th-year classes. Most of the class readers suggested for 1st- and 2nd-year pupils are books specially written for children. The 3rd year is a pivotal stage: there are still suitable books originally written with young readers in mind, but gradually there is a move towards adult books, until in the 4th and 5th years most of the books were originally written for adults. Some of the choices of adult novels may appear dated, and (as with plays) it is difficult to find more recent books which would appeal and which are suitable—usually they are too experimental or too sexually explicit or perverse. It will be interesting to see whether the next decade produces any adult novels with the comparatively wide appeal of those listed here.

1st Year
Dodie Smith, *A Hundred and One Dalmatians*
Rosemary Sutcliff, *Dragonslayer*
Mark Twain, *The Adventures of Tom Sawyer*
John Christopher, *The White Mountains*
Roald Dahl, *Charlie and the Chocolate Factory*
Clive King, *Stig of the Dump*
Helen Cresswell, *The Piemakers*
Bill Naughton, *The Goalkeeper's Revenge*
Meindert DeJong, *The Tower by the Sea*
  The House of Sixty Fathers

2nd Year
Elizabeth Stucley, *Magnolia Buildings*
Ian Serraillier, *The Silver Sword*
Jack London, *White Fang*
Robert C. O'Brien, *Mrs Frisby and the Rats of NIMH*
Peter Dickinson, *The Weathermongers*
A. Rutgers van der Loeff, *The Children on the Oregon Train*
Armstrong Sperry, *The Boy Who Was Afraid*
Pierre Berna, *Flood Warning*
Philippa Pearce, *A Dog So Small*
Scott O'Dell, *The Black Pearl*

3rd Year
Mark Twain, *The Adventures of Huckleberry Finn*
Jack London, *The Call of the Wild*

Wolf Mankowitz, *A Kid for Two Farthings*
The Diary of Anne Frank
H. G. Wells, *The War of the Worlds*
Leon Garfield, *Smith*
Anne Holm, *I Am David*
Ivan Southall, *Hills End*
James Vance Marshall, *Walkabout*
J. Meade Falkner, *Moonfleet*

4th Year
George Orwell, *Animal Farm*
J. D. Salinger, *The Catcher in the Rye*
John Steinbeck, *Of Mice and Men*
   The Pearl
   The Red Pony
Stan Barstow, *Joby*
D. R. Sherman, *Old Mali and the Boy*
Paul Zindel, *The Pigman*
John Wyndham, *The Day of the Triffids*
Jack Schaefer, *Shane*

5th Year
Alan Sillitoe *The Loneliness of the Long Distance Runner*
Keith Waterhouse, *Billy Liar*
   There is a Happy Land
William Golding, *Lord of the Flies*
Laurie Lee, *Cider with Rosie*
Barry Hines, *A Kestrel for a Knave*
Harper Lee, *To Kill a Mocking Bird*
John Le Carré, *The Spy Who Came in from the Cold*
John Braine, *Room at the Top*
John Wyndham, *The Chrysalids*

A. The Reading Lists following each unit in *New English* contain many books which could be used as class readers to follow up and supplement the reading material and ideas given in each unit on a particular theme. It is hoped that pupils will get more literary stimulus than the extracts themselves can provide, and the use of class readers is one way of doing this. Additional oral and written work related to the theme can also emerge from the class reader in the ways suggested above.

Extracts from the selected list of class readers appear in *New English* as follows:
Stan Barstow, *Joby* (NE3, Unit 4)

John Christopher, *The White Mountains* (NE1, Unit 3)
Meindert DeJong, *The Tower by the Sea* (NE1, Unit 7)
The Diary of Anne Frank (NE4, Unit 5)
William Golding, *Lord of the Flies* (NE3, Unit 2)
Barry Hines, *A Kestrel for a Knave* (NE1, Unit 5; NE4, Unit 2, Unit 7)
Anne Holm, *I Am David* (NE2, Unit 9)
Jack London, *The Call of the Wild* (NE2, Unit 8)
   White Fang (NE3, Unit 5)
James Vance Marshall, *Walkabout* (NE3, Unit 3)
Robert C. O'Brien, *Mrs Frisby and the Rats of NIMH* (NE2, Unit 8)
Scott O'Dell, *The Black Pearl* (NE2, Unit 2)
Philippa Pearce, *A Dog So Small* (NE1, Unit 5)
Armstrong Sperry, *The Boy Who Was Afraid* (NE2, Unit 2)
Elizabeth Stucley, *Magnolia Buildings* (NE3, Unit 1)
Rosemary Sutcliff, *Dragonslayer* (NE1, Unit 3)
Mark Twain, *The Adventures of Tom Sawyer* (NE3, Unit 4)
   The Adventures of Huckleberry Finn (NE1, Unit 1)
Keith Waterhouse, *There is a Happy Land* (NE1, Unit 8)
John Wyndham, *The Chrysalids* (NE4, Unit 5)

B. See:
The Reluctant Reader, Aidan Chambers (Pergamon)
Choosing Books for Children, Peter Hollidale (Elek)
Intent upon Reading, Margery Fisher (Brockhampton)
Reading Together, Kenyon Calthrop (Heinemann)
Introducing Books to Children, Aidan Chambers (Heinemann)
   For series of books suitable for use as class readers, see:
Puffins (Penguin)
The New Windmill Series (Heinemann)
Imprint Books (Longman)
The Heritage of Literature Series (Longman)
Pleasure in Reading (Longman)
Topliners (Macmillan)

C. See also CHILDREN'S LITERATURE, NOVELS, PLAYS, READING ALOUD, SHORT STORIES, SILENT READING.

Clause Analysis

Is there any point in clause analysis—in finding finite verbs and distinguishing main clauses from subordinate clauses and deciding whether a clause is adjectival, adverbial, or noun? There is some point, I think, but not too much.

It isn't necessary to know very much about how a motor car works in order to be able to drive it. It isn't necessary to know how sentences are constructed in order to be able to write. But if the car goes wrong or if the writing goes wrong, then it is useful to know something about the mechanics in order to put it right or to improve the performance. If a pupil knows something about cause analysis, then it is possible to explain why this is not a sentence or why that doesn't make sense or how a series of simple sentences can be more interestingly expressed or why something is considered grammatically incorrect.

Clause analysis should at least get pupils to look more closely at sentences, just as dictionary work or vocabulary exercises get them to look at words. Words and sentences are the basic material with which ideas and concepts are expressed. Without some awareness of how they work, of the variety available and of the different nuances of meaning, which can be produced by using them effectively, then a pupil's writing and understanding will remain on an elementary level, depending for its success on intuitive skill or insight.

That at least is the theory. Clause analysis should enable pupils to read more profitably by enabling them to see where a sentence is taking them. It should lead them to use more complicated and more neatly constructed and more varied sentences themselves. But is there, in fact, any carry-over from analysis into understanding and writing? It is difficult to say and impossible to prove.

Do writers really think like that? Do they decide, 'Ah, now I need an adjectival clause' or, 'A nice noun clause is needed to introduce this sentence'? Probably not. But they may well think things like these: 'A simple statement of fact would start this paragraph off well' or, 'A series of simple sentences would help to build up the suspense' or, 'This is very disjointed: it would be more fluent if I made these three sentences into one.'

So how are we to encourage pupils to adopt this kind of critical approach to what they write and, by transference, to what they read? One possible way ('possible' only) is through clause analysis—by close examination of how sentences work.

Some pupils take to clause analysis easily; others never get the hang of it. What has to be evaluated is the balance of effort required to profit achieved. There is no point in doing exercise after exercise in the determination to make sure that all pupils understand all the niceties: for some of them this day will never come. Instead, all one can do is bring the various aspects of clause analysis to their attention step by step, try to help them to understand them, give them some practice in distinguishing them, and leave it at that. Some pupils may appreciate it and find it useful in their writing or in working out what Henry James or Shakespeare is getting at in a particular piece of writing through examining the various clauses; some may find it an interesting game akin to a jigsaw or a crossword puzzle; others will be bewildered and unable to master one aspect sufficiently to go on to the next.

Once, clause analysis was an essential and frequently repeated part of English teaching; many pupils today never come anywhere near clause analysis. Perhaps it is time for some kind of middle course where clause analysis is seen, not as boring and meaningless exercise, but as a means of examining more precisely how sentences work and how writers write.

A. Much of the work of the Language sections of NE3 is taken up with the analysis of sentence structure, taking pupils step by step from simple sentences to more complicated ones.

C. See also GRAMMAR, SENTENCES.

Comic Verse

For many pupils, comic verse is the only kind of poetry they read with genuine enjoyment, and certainly the only kind of poetry most of them are prepared to read for themselves. Teachers should take advantage of the appeal that comic verse has and use as much of it as possible in their lessons, particularly with younger pupils. You never know, something may get across to the pupils, and they may be less resistant to more serious poetry when they have had some experience of actively enjoying comic verse in the past. Care in the choice of poems is essential as tastes change and much light verse is too sophisticated or too literary for young people. Selections from the following poets usually go down well: Ogden Nash, Spike Milligan, Michael Rosen, Charles Causley, John Betjeman, Roger McGough.

Writing comic verse of their own can also act as a lead-in to other writing. Using simple verse forms like the clerihew, the limerick, the riddle, the haiku, and the epitaph can provide pleasant lessons where verbal manipulation and a bit of ingenuity can be rewarded by agreeable results. This again may provide some perhaps primitive understanding of rhythm, rhyme, and verse form which may carry over to more serious poetry in both reading and writing.

A. Some suggestions for writing comic verse are given in NE1, Unit 4, and NE2, Unit 4.

B. The following anthologies of comic verse can provide useful material:

Here Lies, ed. Robert Millar (Heinemann)
Verse and Worse, ed. Arnold Silcock (Faber)
The Penguin Book of Comic and Curious Verse, ed. J. M. Cohen
More Comic and Curious Verse, ed. J. M. Cohen (Penguin)
Yet More Comic and Curious Verse, ed. J. M. Cohen (Penguin)
Parodies, ed. Dwight Macdonald (Faber)
The Lure of the Limerick (Pan)
A Dustbin of Milligan (Tandem)
The New Oxford Book of Light Verse, ed. Kingsley Amis (OUP)
The Faber Book of Comic Verse, ed. Michael Roberts (Faber)
Meet My Folks, Ted Hughes (Faber)
The Batsford Book of Light Verse for Children, ed. Gavin Ewart (Batsford)

C. See also POETRY, WRITING POETRY.

Compendiums

When displaying work or publishing work in a class or school magazine, it is often possible to collate extracts from a number of pieces written by different pupils to build up a composite article which presents a more interesting picture than a single individual piece of writing would do. It also provides an opportunity for a large number of pupils to have their work noticed, and even the weaker pupils are capable of writing a couple of sentences which could be quoted where their complete pieces do not have that merit. Subjects such as my pets, my favourite food, my hobbies, how I spend Saturday morning, my ideal holiday, and where I live can be selected from in this way, and a kind of survey of the class's general interests and tastes produced.

A. Compendiums of this kind can be found in *New English* as follows:

A Class Portrait, NE1, Unit 1
Meet Our Pets, NE1, Unit 5
Holidays, NE1, Unit 9
Food and Drink, NE3, Unit 3
The Police, NE4, Unit 6

Comprehension

Research some years ago suggested that practice in comprehension exercises had little effect on the performance in a comprehension exercise in an examination: candidates who had done no practice achieved just as good results.

However, I feel that that does not necessarily invalidate comprehension exercises. Answering questions on a passage at least forces the pupil to look more closely at the passage, and to formulate, organize and communicate his understanding of the passage. Answers can be oral or written, providing practice in these skills, and questions can explore what actually happens in the passage or the implications of the passage or lead beyond it to issues raised by the passage. While there are times when a general understanding or simple enjoyment are sufficient, there are also times when a detailed examination, precise understanding and close analysis are valid. A pupil's progress is going to be slow or haphazard if it is to be taken for granted that he understands everything he reads. There must be times when a pupil's appreciation is tested and when his attention is directed towards specific points by means of questions. Too frequent or inappropriate questioning can undermine the pleasure of reading, but no questioning at all can mean that pupils rarely penetrate beneath the surface.

Some comprehension questions will inevitably be of a kind where there is only one correct answer, for instance where factual information is required about what is actually happening in the passage; but many questions should be more open, allowing for differences in interpretation, calling upon a personal response from the pupils, or allowing them to relate the questions and the passage to their own experience. This latter type is just as valuable in testing whether the passage has been understood; by exploring his own experience, the pupil's appreciation of the passage can be deepened.

Different types of writing should be studied in this way—prose, verse, statistics, graphs, instructions, forms, letters, reportage, propaganda. Possibly the most important reading many pupils will be called upon to undertake in later life will be the interpretation of instructions or the filling in of forms, so close analysis of types of writing of these kinds at this stage through comprehension exercises may help them to cope more adequately.

A. Each unit in *New English* contains comprehension exercises. These may be taken orally or they may be written. The passages may be read for enjoyment or used to start off a discussion, and the questions ignored.

More specific guidance on how to approach comprehension exercises in examinations is given in NE4, Units 3 and 4.

Consolidation

Every teacher knows that you can't say something once and expect every pupil to hear it, understand it, and learn it. Pupils are imperfect receivers with their sets turned off or faulty. Therefore, repetition is inevitable. Things like the use of the apostrophe, the use of capital letters, the punctuation of speech, correct sentence construction, etc., have to be gone over at regular intervals in the hope that each time a few more pupils will understand.

A. There are regular Consolidation sections in *New English* designed to test what has been learned in previous units. These concentrate on language, vocabulary, and spelling. They could be used as tests in class to check on whether the material has been understood and learned, as monitoring exercises, and as revision of sections which it is clear have not been grasped.

Some topics, such as parts of speech, sentence structure, punctuation, and figures of speech, are repeated in the course of the four books as it is felt that to deal with them once and expect them to be learned is unrealistic.

Correction of Work

The ideal method of correcting the written work of a pupil is to go over the piece of writing with the individual pupil by your side. In this way, it is possible to point to a line in which there is a mistake in spelling or punctuation, and the pupil himself is usually able to see the mistake and to correct it. It is also possible to discuss the writing with the pupil, to comment on its merits and defects and to suggest improvements. Clearly, it is not possible to do this with all the work that is done, but some time in the week should be found for this kind of approach (perhaps during silent reading periods or writing periods) and every pupil in the class should receive this individual attention with the opportunity it gives for a consideration of his own particular technical mistakes at least once a term.

The more common method of correcting work is to collect it, mark it at home, and return it with corrections and comments. The problem here is to ensure that the pupil looks at and learns from the corrections. It sometimes feels that marking is a self-imposed masochistic exercise on the part of the teacher as many pupils rarely bother to look at the corrections and are only interested in the final mark or comment—if that. Perhaps insisting on corrections being written out by the pupil would help or the keeping of spelling note-books, but this provides something else which the teacher has to chase and check up on, and it requires a fairly rigid organization and routine.

Should marking be comprehensive or selective? Should every single mistake be circled in red ink or only the most blatant? The drawback to the first approach is that a page covered in red marks could have a depressing effect on a pupil who has been eager to communicate and may inhibit him from writing so freely in the future. There is also some doubt as to whether a pupil whose work contains so many mistakes would be able to distinguish between them in a mass of corrections and learn from them. The difficulty with the second approach is that parents and colleagues in other departments may have their worst fears confirmed: that is, that the English department doesn't bother about spelling any more.

A possible compromise would be to mark the first paragraph fairly intensively and then only incidental mistakes subsequently. Or distinguish between pieces of writing where fluency and interest and imagination are important which would be lightly corrected and pieces of writing where particular attention is to be paid to technical correctness.

Opinions vary about the kind of mark that should be affixed to a piece of writing. Should it be a mark out of twenty, a grade, or an estimate which appears in the markbook but not on the pupil's work? Should the piece of writing be graded against the teacher's knowledge of the pupil's individual standard, or should it be on an objective scale indicating the level of achievement of the pupil compared with others in his age-group? There is no single or simple answer here.

Probably, since encouragement and praise are more likely to produce improvement than criticism and reproof, a pupil's work should be evaluated against his own previous efforts so that it is possible for a weak pupil to get a top grade because he has produced a good piece of work for him.

This approach certainly applies to the kind of comments made on a pupil's work. These should be constructive not destructive. They should convey the reader's appreciation and enjoyment. The pupil in his writing is communicating with *you* and if you always reject what he has written because it is badly phrased or incorrectly punctuated, then it will hardly be surprising if the pupil grows reluctant to communicate with you any more. The best form of encouragement and incentive is to read the best work out to the rest of the class. This can also indicate to the class the kind of standard you expect and the kind of standard pupils should be aspiring to. Nor need this always be the work of the brightest pupils: a teacher's reading can often conceal the deficiencies of spelling and punctuation in the work of a weak pupil to reveal the liveliness and interest obscured beneath.

Some teachers and departments evolve elaborate sets of symbols to be used in correcting work to indicate different kinds of mistakes. For example, / may indicate a spelling mistake, X a punctuation mistake, etc. It may be a system worth considering, although again its success would depend on having a fairly rigid routine in the classroom where whenever written work is returned pupils are required to sit down and go through it putting in the corrections. There may be value in occasionally marking work by simply putting crosses in the margin against every line containing a mistake and asking pupils to correct the work.

Another method of following through on work that has been corrected is for the teacher to make a list of words commonly misspelled or constructions incorrectly used to act as the basis for a lesson. With examples taken from pupils' work, there is the possibility that pupils will pay more attention to the discussion, and the points made will be directly relevant to the pupils' needs.

Marking work is one of the burdens which teachers of English have to a greater degree than teachers of other subjects. The sheer volume of written work which has to be gone through can be intimidating. One method of lightening the load is to avoid over-marking: there is no need to correct every single mistake. Another is to vary the intensity of the marking: mark the first paragraph fully, and then 'impression read' the rest. Not all the marking can be done in free periods or at home; some time has to be found in the classroom, going over work with individual pupils, or marking while pupils are engaged in some task. Occasionally, pupils could be asked to mark each other's work: this can be a useful exercise in observation and criticism. It may be worthwhile sometimes reproducing a piece of work by a pupil so that each pupil has a copy and going through it looking at and commenting on mistakes. But no matter what methods are used, marking will form a major part of the English teacher's role.

Much of the time is taken up with correcting careless mistakes, slips of the pen, points which could have been corrected by the pupil himself if he had bothered to check over his work, or with the minutiae of full stops omitted or words incorrectly spelled. It is more difficult to get down to what may be considered more important things such as improvements in style or structure of a piece of writing. This can be more easily done in private discussion with an individual pupil or through general discussion on a piece that has been read out or which has been reproduced for the whole class. More attention to aspects like these can perhaps be encouraged by asking pupils to write rough versions first or to rewrite work that has been corrected. But the fact that first thoughts are not necessarily the best and that any good piece of writing usually has to be chopped and changed and rewritten before it begins to approach an ideal completed version is a difficult concept to communicate to pupils. The idea that W. B. Yeats wrote his poems fifty times before he was satisfied with them—if then—is one that pupils find strange and incomprehensible. But it is nevertheless one which the teacher has to keep placing before his pupils if genuine progress is to be made.

C.   See also ASSESSMENT, SENTENCES, SPELLING, WRITING.

Course Books

The main objections to course books are that they are created in a vacuum and may not be relevant to the needs or interests of a particular class, and that they exclude the teacher, to a greater or lesser extent, from responsibility for and involvement with the work of the class.

The value of course books lies in the fact that they can provide material for lessons based on a degree of preparation and research that the teacher himself may not have time for; they can provide the non-specialist teacher of English with some kind of security; they need not be followed through religiously page by page, but can be adapted by the teacher to the requirements of his teaching; and even page by page, they may be more effective than a bad teacher.

Course books vary tremendously in quality and in intention. It would be a useful exercise for student teachers (and practising teachers) to examine and evaluate a number of current course books to see how effective or useful they would be. It has always seemed strange that Colleges of Education rarely include any study of the books their students may well actually use in the classroom. An important (and financially responsible) part of any teacher's job is to recommend and buy books for his classes, yet training in this is seldom given.

A.   *New English* is designed as a course book for mixed ability classes leading to CSE or 'O' Level (although NEC is recommended for the final stage of a purely 'O' Level group). The work is divided into separate units, each based on a particular theme. In each unit, there are sections on reading and understanding, writing, language work, vocabulary, and spelling. Suggestions for further reading are included, and there are many opportunities for oral work. An attempt has been made to keep a balance between literature and language work. The extracts from novels, particularly in the first three books, have been chosen mainly from the work of authors who write specifically for young people (such as William Mayne, Philippa Pearce, and Rosemary Sutcliff). Extracts from 'classics' such as *Jane Eyre* and *Robinson Crusoe* have also been included as well as much writing by young people themselves. The extracts are deliberately of a good length so that there is enough meat for pupils to get their teeth into. The course is intentionally demanding, and some pupils may find some sections difficult, but it is hoped that the teacher will adapt and organize the material to the needs of his pupils as well as supplement it with material of his own.

B.   A comparison of the following course books could be interesting. They are not necessarily all recommended.

New English, Rhodri Jones (Heinemann)

English Through Experience, Albert Rowe and Peter Emmens (Hart Davis)

Explore and Express, R. M. Adams, J. L. Foster, and R. L. Wilson (Macmillan)

Actions and Reactions, Maureen Stewart and Terry Doyle (Macmillan)

Action in English, Rony Robinson and W. T. Cunningham (Nelson)

Mainstream English, J. R. C. Yglesias and L. E. Snellgrove (Longman)

Contemporary English, John Foster (Macmillan)

Looking into English, Peter Emmens (Hart Davis)

I've Got to Use Words, David Holbrooke (CUP)

Interplay, John Watts (Longman)

The Art of English, Keith Newson (Schofield and Sims)

Living Expression, J. Hodgson and E. Richards (Ginn)

C.   See also ANTHOLOGIES.

Course Work

For the CSE examination, pupils are required to present a folder of course work, representing the best work they have done during the two years of the course, and the grade given for this work contributes towards the final result. The presentation of this folder—with the work neatly written out and with a contents page—is important. This is something which can be encouraged lower down the school, especially if the thematic approach is used and work is done on loose-leaf sheets and kept in folders. At the end of a theme or topic, pupils could be asked to arrange their work in order and to provide a front cover using pictures or drawings and a contents page. A mark for the whole theme could then be assigned. This is one way of finishing off a theme, and it also helps pupils to get into the habit of arranging and organizing their work.

A.   See NE4, Unit 1, on course work.

C.   See also CERTIFICATE OF SECONDARY EDUCATION EXAMINATION, THEMES.

Creative Writing

Recent years have seen a tremendous increase in interest in creative writing by children, and a number of collections of this kind of writing have been published. There has been a danger of over-rating this writing, of seeing in it an innocence and purity and imaginative power simply because it is the work of young people. A sense of proportion is necessary. Children's writing can often be original and striking, but it is mainly interesting because of the very fact that it is children's writing not because it equals the subtleties or insights of adult literature.

Another danger has been that teachers have seen this kind of writing as the only valid kind of writing for pupils to undertake, and English lessons have become intensive writers' workshops. Again, a sense of balance is necessary. Creative writing is valid because it can encourage personal growth and development through stimulating pupils to write about what it would feel like to be other people or to be in situations other than their own or to explore their own experience more deeply or to use their imaginations and senses. But other forms of writing are also important and must be practised.

Much good creative writing comes out of a study of what other people have written. A good short story or an extract from a novel or a poem can illuminate a situation or an emotion, and pupils can use this illumination as an inspiration for their own writing. Discussion on its own, or the personal experience of others, can act as a starting point. The use of stimuli like pictures or music or an appeal to the senses can equally create the right conditions out of which good creative writing can emerge.

A. *New English* contains many examples of creative writing by young people. These are listed in the indexes of each volume. Writing assignments, many of which are creative in nature, and which often arise out of the poems and extracts used, are included in each unit.

B. For further examples of creative writing by young people, see the following:
Children as Writers (Heinemann)
The Keen Eye, Jack Beckett (Blackie)
Young Writers, Young Readers, ed. Boris Ford (Hutchinson)
Children as Poets, ed. Denys Thompson (Heinemann)
The World in a Classroom, ed. Chris Searle (Writers and Readers Publishing Cooperative)
Enjoying Writing, A. B. Clegg (Hart Davis)
Imagine, eds. Robert Protherough and John Smith (Harrap)
   School magazines and the work of the English Centre, Ebury Teachers' Centre, Sutherland Street, London, SW1 provide other sources.

C. See also MUSIC, PICTURES, STIMULUS, WRITING, WRITING POETRY.

Debates

An occasional formal debate with a motion, a chairman, a proposer, opposer, and seconders can make a useful change from class discussion and can impose order on what might otherwise be desultory and formless. The discipline of having to prepare a speech, stand up and deliver it, and reply to any questions raised is a valuable experience. Similarly, the need to see the holes in an opponent's arguments sharpens the critical sense. Probably it is wiser for the teacher to act as chairman unless he is lucky enough to have an exceptionally articulate pupil with a strong personality who can control the proceedings. A debate also provides a good excuse for rearranging the furniture in the classroom and getting pupils out of the serried ranks of desks.

A. Some suggestions for debates are given in the Activities sections of *New English*.

C. See also DISCUSSION, ORAL WORK, SPEECHES, TALK.

Departmental Meetings

For some departments, with two or three members, departmental meetings may not be necessary; but with English departments, which tend to be large, they are vital if the department is to work cohesively and achieve its full potential. Informal meetings between members of the department over coffee during break or casual chat about pupils and lessons and books is not enough. Formal departmental meetings with an agenda and minutes and full discussion are essential for the smooth running and purposeful organization of the department.

Departmental meetings should be policy-making occasions. They provide the opportunity for all members of the department to contribute and to be consulted. It is very important that even the most junior member of the department should feel able to have his say and to feel that he is contributing to the policy of the team. He should also be able to benefit from the experience of the others. It is the variety of points of view and experiences which can be expressed in the thrashing out of a common policy which may be so valuable.

Clearly, various organizational matters will have to be discussed, such as the introduction of new books, decisions about examination entries, the allocation of classes. But the real meat of departmental meetings should be discussion and decisions on matters of policy such as examinations (Are they necessary in the lower and middle school?); spelling (Should we bother with it or not?); setting (Should we teach in mixed ability groups?) The aims of English teaching and the revision and keeping up to date of the syllabus are matters that all members of the department should have the opportunity to comment on.

One way of initiating discussion is to request a member of the department to present a paper on a given topic. Another useful way is to invite an English teacher from another school to give his views or talk from his experience, or a member of another department, such as remedial or modern languages who could say where he thought the English department could make a contribution to his teaching.

The County or Borough Advisor for English can also be involved here by attending meetings to describe new approaches or to comment on practice in other schools. Working papers that can be used as a starting point are published by the National Association for the Teaching of English in its journal *English in Education* (in association with Oxford University Press). Articles in *The Use of English* (available from the Scottish Academic Press, 33 Montgomery Street, Edinburgh EH7 5JX) can also be used to set off discussion at a departmental meeting and to help formulate departmental policy.

The head of department's role in meetings like this can be either to initiate discussion on new policy or to act as chairman so that all complexions of opinion can be aired. He has to make final decisions, but he should take into account the general feeling of his colleagues.

It is important that something concrete should come out of meetings and that the points raised and the discussion generated should not simply be allowed to evaporate. This could take the form of minutes or policy documents and a body of departmental practice can be built up. This can be useful for reference, helpful in the running of the department and valuable to a new member of the department in putting him in the picture.

If diversity of views are allowed an airing and diplomatically handled, departmental meetings can increase teachers' morale and help to encourage a unity of purpose and a sense of direction.

B. See:
Head of Department, Michael Marland (Heinemann)

C. See also AIMS OF ENGLISH TEACHING, HEAD OF DEPARTMENT, SYLLABUS.

Dialect

The local dialect deserves considerable attention in the classroom. It provides an immediate and interesting source for linguistic study, and pupils may well be able to inform the teacher for a change. Aspects of vocabulary, pronunciation, grammatical constructions, and popular sayings should be looked at and examples collected. Pupils should be encouraged to write or tape-record pieces in their local dialect. The differences between dialect and standard English should be noted, and examples of other dialects studied. Literature in the local dialect or in other dialects can be read. As a project, this could yield exciting results, and it is one in which pupils are more likely to be involved than some other kinds of language work.

It is important to stress that dialect is an alternative kind of language to standard English, not necessarily an inferior one: it is a question of where and how it is used. Many pupils use one kind of language in the playground and another in the classroom, and the reasons behind this fact could be discussed, as well as the questions of snobbery in language, class, and accents.

A. Dialect is discussed and illustrated in NE1, Unit 1, and in NE4, Unit 5. Many of the extracts used are in dialect form or contain dialogue in a particular dialect, and these would repay study. See, for instance:

The Adventures of Huckleberry Finn, Mark Twain (NE1, Unit 1)
London Labour and London Poor, Henry Mayhew (NE2 Unit 8; NE4, Unit 6)
Magnolia Buildings, Elizabeth Stucley (NE3, Unit 1)
Tam O'Shanter, Robert Burns (NE1, Unit 7)
A Kestrel for a Knave, Barry Hines (NE1, Unit 5; NE4, Units 2 and 7)
The Lonely Londoners, Samuel Selvon (NE4, Unit 5)

B. See also:
They Don't Speak Our Language, ed. Sinclair Rogers (Arnold)
Accent, Dialect and the School, Peter Trudgill (Arnold)
English Dialects, G. L. Brook (Andre Deutsch)
The West Indian Language Issue in British Schools, U.K. Edwards (RKP)

C. See also MULTI-RACIAL ENGLISH, PRONUNCIATION, STANDARD ENGLISH.

Dialogue

Dialogue is something most pupils want to use in their stories, so teaching the punctuation of speech is essential. The mechanics are quite complicated, and a number of sessions of going over the rules will probably be necessary. Studying a conversation in a book can also help. As practice, pupils can be asked to write a simple dialogue between two characters—a traffic warden and a motorist, for example, or a shopkeeper and an awkward customer. Many pupils find the punctuation of speech difficult, and it is quite likely that a number of them will never get the hang of it.

At the danger of confusing pupils, short scenes or plays could be written where the punctuation of speech is not necessary. As an exercise, part of these could then be translated into a story where speech marks are required.

Some discussion of the kind of dialogue useful in writing could be valuable. It should be dialogue that furthers the action or reveals character, not idle chat about the weather or enquiries about health. The study of some dialogue in a piece of good writing would be constructive here.

A. The mechanics of punctuating dialogue are discussed in NE2, Unit 3, and NE4, Unit 3. Many of the extracts contain dialogue that could be useful in demonstrating how it works.

Dictation

In theory, writing down a passage from dictation should train pupils to interpret the sound of words in visual terms and to become more aware of punctuation. Whether this works in practice or not is another matter. It is worth trying occasionally as a change, and pupils sometimes enjoy it. Perhaps the real value comes in asking pupils to correct each other's versions when their observation of what is actually on the written page can be tested.

A. No passages for dictation as such are given in *New English*, but almost any extract could be used for this purpose. As a test of whether spellings have been learned, the teacher could devise sentences containing words from the current spelling list.

B. *Alpha to Omega* by Bevé Hornsby and Frula Shear (Heinemann) contains many sentences and passages intended for dictation. These are clearly allied to particular spellings and groups of words and would therefore have more relevance than passages chosen at random simply for the purpose of dictation.

C. See also SPELLING.

Dictionary

Every pupil should have practice in using a dictionary, and every effort should be made to encourage pupils to get into the habit of referring to a dictionary as need arises. This has to be done from the very beginning of a pupil's school career and, if possible, each pupil should have his own dictionary or have access to one. Some schools make it a requirement or suggestion that all new entrants in the first year should provide their own dictionaries as the cost for the school to buy dictionaries for all pupils is prohibitive.

A lesson simply explaining the kind of information a dictionary can give is useful to start with, and the teacher could devise exercises intended to do this. For instance, finding out the parts of speech of particular words, pronunciation, different meanings, idiomatic phrases, derivations, additional words formed from a particular root, words containing a particular prefix or suffix.

Other lessons could be devoted to expanding on each of these aspects in turn: exercises intended to extend vocabulary, comprehension exercises based on a particular word or a particular page. Interesting words to look at would be 'do', 'make', 'be', 'see', 'bank', 'blow', 'bear', 'press', 'mark', 'crown', 'go', 'tear'.

There may even be some point in giving lists of words for pupils to find out the meaning of and then use in sentences of their own, though it is always better for the words to come from a particular context, a passage the pupils are reading, rather than being presented in isolation.

A. Many of the Vocabulary sections in *New English* suggest the use of dictionaries, and most of the extracts could be used to provide words for dictionary practice. The use of the dictionary is specifically referred to in NE1, Unit 1, NE2, Unit 1, NE3, Unit 1, NE4, Unit 1.

B. The following dictionaries could be recommended for use by pupils:
The Oxford School Dictionary (OUP)
The Pocket Oxford Dictionary (OUP)
The Nelson Contemporary English Dictionary (Nelson)
English Dictionary (Penguin)
Heinemann English Dictionary (Heinemann)
Chambers Students' English Dictionary (Chambers)

C. See also REFERENCE BOOKS, SPELLING, VOCABULARY.

Discussion

Pupils must have the opportunity to express their views on a wide variety of subjects and to listen to the views of other people. Discussion can arise as an integral part of the work of the class (as an introduction to a theme to be studied such as 'Parents' or 'Work', as a preparation for writing, or as a follow-on of comprehension). It can also arise from events of importance in the school or in the news (and often 'spontaneous' discussions such as these can be the most natural and the most valuable).

The teacher's role as initiator is important. He can also provide information and suggest alternative views or draw out some evidence for statements made or bring in people who are not contributing. Usually, comments have to go through the teacher as chairman in order to preserve control, but ideally, the teacher should merely be one of the group having his say like the others, and pupils should respond to each other directly without having to use the teacher as an intermediary. This is more likely to be possible in group discussion with five or six members of the class in each group. Pupils should have practice in chairing and taking minutes for their group, and there should be a general session in which the 'secretaries' of the groups report back to the class as a whole.

The teacher's attitude in discussion is vital. No pupil is going to express his opinions unless he feels that what he has to say will be respected and listened to. The teacher must create an atmosphere in which each contribution is seen to be valuable, even if he has to filter out the information or clarify the point of view being expressed. Sarcasm or impatience or harsh criticism will stifle spontaneity and the willingness to talk.

Listening is as important as talking, and the teacher must ensure that there is the right kind of control in the classroom. A situation where everyone is talking and no one listening is futile; a rigidly imposed silence which inhibits people from contributing is equally destructive. The right kind of balance is difficult to achieve. It depends on the personality of the teacher, the kind of relationship he has built up with the class, the skill with which a subject is chosen for its interest and relevance and with which the discussion is conducted, the clear statement of and insistence on certain rules for the orderly running of a discussion—such as that one person speaks at a time. (The function of the conch in William Golding's *Lord of the Flies* might be a useful illustration here.) The arrangement of the furniture in the classroom may also be relevant—a situation where pupils are sitting round in a circle and everyone can see who is speaking is likely to be more successful in maintaining interest than where pupils are sitting at desks all facing the front. Some time for thought and preparation and even the writing of notes may also help to ensure that pupils have something to say and want to say it.

A. All the units in *New English* provide ample opportunities for discussion, either incidentally or as the basis for a complete lesson.

C. See also DEBATES, GROUP WORK, ORAL WORK, SKILLS, TALK.

Display

The use of display material in the classroom can help to create a more human and lived-in environment. Posters and pictures are obvious examples of material which can be used, but newspaper articles and pictures, poems and work by pupils are other sources. This is particularly valuable if you are doing thematic work where a display of appropriate newspaper cuttings and pictures and pieces of work by pupils on the theme can help to build up interest and can act as motivation. If pupils are asked to find poems on a particular theme, these could be written out and displayed to form a kind of anthology. They help to decorate the walls, they help to convey the sense of activity in the classroom, and you never know, someone might actually read them.

The use of pupils' work in display can encourage the pupils whose work is chosen, and it provides a good reason for asking pupils to write their work out again neatly so that other people can read it. This material, when taken down, can be stored and used to show the work of the English department on parents' evenings or open days, or it can provide material for a class or school magazine.

A. Many opportunities for collecting material for display are suggested in the Activities sections of *New English*.

C. See also ACTIVITIES, ANTHOLOGIES, MAGAZINE, THEMES.

Drama

It is not within the scope of this book to discuss the role of drama in education in depth, but since it is an essential part of English teaching, it is important that teachers of English are aware of its relevance, take pains to develop it, and provide opportunities for their pupils to take part in it.

Drama allows the chance for a different kind of self-expression. If the development of the skills of speech and writing are important, then so is the development of expression through movement and 'speech in action'. By acting out a situation, pupils can often learn about it and show a deeper awareness of the implications of that situation. Often they are able to show an understanding of the situation through improvisation that is more mature than they could achieve simply by talking or writing about it. Through imagining and showing the feelings of other people, pupils can learn more about themselves. This 'personal growth' aspect of drama is one of the main contributions drama makes to English teaching.

44

Some pupils have a particular skill in improvisation and may have a success in drama which is denied them in other aspects of English. It is important for them that they should have the chance to shine, and that their peers should appreciate their skill in this aspect.

The content of drama appropriate for the classroom can be divided into different areas. There are drama exercises whose main purpose is to increase discipline or observation or sensitivity. These may take the form of imagining a crumpled piece of paper is a bird and handing it carefully round the class or responding to the mood of a piece of music. Often exercises of this kind can be utilized when it comes to the second type of drama that can be used in the classroom— improvisation. A situation is set up in general terms by the teacher—it might be a family row or people getting into trouble. The pupils in groups then discuss the situation and work out a story which illustrates it. They invent and develop characters and incidents. They adapt and organize the acting space using whatever furniture or props are available. They rehearse their improvisation and then present it for the rest of the class to see and discuss. This kind of activity is probably the main one in drama lessons.

There are other 'non-dramatic' activities which may be valid in drama lessons, things like discussions, debates, prepared talks or demonstrations, games and quizzes, interviews, tape recordings, prepared readings, radio programmes. There are also scripted plays. There is certainly a place for these in drama lessons—either printed plays or scripts which pupils have worked on and written themselves—but there is always the problem of what to do with pupils who do not have speaking or acting parts. There is a limit to the number of jobs like stage manager, prompter, props assistant that can be devised. The proper place for scripted plays is probably as an after-school activity where those interested can be fully involved.

Order and control are essential in drama lessons. Too often, if organization is weak, lessons can deteriorate into chaos and opportunities for pupils—and sometimes teachers—to be merely self-indulgent. It is the responsibility of the teacher to provide the control and organization and to present the stimulus, whether it be music, a piece of literature, the outlining of a mood or a situation, in such a way as to inspire pupils to think deeply about it and to respond to it. After an improvisation, discussion and criticism are vital as it is out of this that a great deal of the value of drama can emerge: pupils have explored the experience through preparing and performing the improvisation; now they should try to put into words what they have learned. It is also possible that written work could emerge from improvisation and be part of the drama lesson.

A vital element of good organization is having a reasonable place in which the drama lesson can take place. A normal classroom with the desks pushed back won't do: you need a large uncluttered space. Rostra and chairs and pieces of furniture which can be arranged and adapted as required by pupils in their improvisations are useful. Other equipment could include some spotlights, masks, quantities of assorted items of dress, unusual objects (such as a sheep's skull or part of a machine), a tape-recorder, a record player, cameras.

Educational drama and theatre are sometimes seen as diametrically opposed activities, but there is no reason why drama in the classroom should not be used to encourage an interest in theatre and theatrical performance. It is even possible that the one could be used to sharpen an interest in and an awareness of the qualities of the other. Similarly, educational drama can spill over into film and television. Discussion about what is currently on show can lead to improvisations or to the making of films or television programmes if the equipment and technical expertise are available.

A. Suggestions for drama work are contained in the Activities sections of *New English*.

B. See the following for much more detailed accounts of the philosophy and practice of educational drama:
Drama and Theatre in Education, ed. Nigel Dodd and Winifred Hickson (Heinemann)
100+ Ideas for Drama, Anna Scher and Charles Verrall (Heinemann)
A Practical Guide to Drama in the Secondary School, David Self (Ward Lock)
Theatre for Youth, Robert Leach (Wheaton)
Creative Drama in Schools, Gabriel Barnfield (Macmillan)
An Introduction to Child Drama, Peter Slade (Hodder and Stoughton)
Development Through Drama, Brian Way (Longman)
Dorothy Heathcote: Drama as a Learning Medium, Betty Jane Wagner (National Education Association)
Improvisation, John Hodgson and Ernest Richards (Eyre Methuen)
The Uses of Drama, John Hodgson (Eyre Methuen)

C. See also ACTIVITIES, ORAL WORK, PLAYS, SCHOOL PLAY, VISITS.

Duplicating Material

No textbook contains, exactly, all the material necessary for or appropriate to the requirements of a particular class. Inevitably there will be a poem or a newspaper article or a set of statistics which the teacher needs for a lesson which is not readily available in a school textbook, and he will have to type it out and duplicate it or photocopy it. This provision of resource material which the teacher has found for himself and which is exactly right for the class at that precise moment is part of what being a good teacher is about. It means extra work, but it is also likely to mean more stimulating teaching.

Ideally, the duplicated material should be attractive and as durable as possible, but unfortunately, not many schools have off-set litho equipment or photocopiers or laminating machines. But every school must have some kind of duplicating equipment, and it is worth the effort of using it. Where there is a convenient teachers' centre, it may be possible to use the resources for duplicating and making material which are available there.

Possibly, material duplicated like this could be kept in a central store so that other teachers in the department can use it. With each teacher contributing, a large body of resource material can be built up without putting the burden of the work too much on the shoulders of one individual.

C. See also RESOURCES, STOCK ROOM, TEACHERS' CENTRE.

English Literature

See ADVANCED LEVEL, HERITAGE OF ENGLISH LITERATURE, ORDINARY LEVEL.

Equipment

The basic equipment for a teacher of English consists of chalk and talk and books and paper. However, there are other technical aids which can provide more sophisticated resources and assistance. Some kind of equipment for duplicating material is essential whether it be a spirit copier or a photocopier. Access to a typewriter, a tape recorder, a cassette recorder, a radio, a television, and a record player is also desirable. Another item that can be useful is a projector for transparencies, slides, film-strips, and films. A polaroid camera can provide stimulating material. Further discussion of this topic could be the basis for an item at a departmental meeting.

47

Advantage should also be taken of equipment which may be available from other sources such as a teachers' centre, a local college of education, a local theatre or arts centre. Many children have their own recording facilities, and it is very useful to tap this immediate resource.

C. See also DRAMA, DUPLICATING MATERIAL, RESOURCES, SPECIALIST CLASSROOMS.

Examinations

Public examinations are discussed under CERTIFICATE OF SECONDARY EDUCATION, ORDINARY LEVEL and ADVANCED LEVEL. The extent to which these external examinations determine the content of the teaching of English is something which each English department will have to decide for itself. (See AIMS OF ENGLISH TEACHING.)

Is there a need for internal examinations in English? They could act as an incentive to read and study set texts or provide an opportunity to do some writing or help to distinguish between those doing CSE and those doing 'O' Level. In the later stages, they can also give pupils practice in sitting examinations in preparation for their final tests. I feel, though, that examinations are not necessary in the earlier years of the secondary school. The teacher should not need examinations to find out whether particular pupils are making progress or not: he will know from the work the pupil does week by week. There may be a need for the English department to set examinations if they are set in other subjects in order to maintain 'parity of esteem', but this is something again which individual English departments could discuss.

A. *New English* is designed as a preparation for CSE and 'O' Level English Language examinations. For 'O' Level, NEC may be preferred.

There are regular Consolidation sections which test some of the material discussed and studied in previous units. These could be a useful way of revising work, checking if it has been understood, and allowing pupils to catch up.

C. See also ADVANCED LEVEL, AIMS OF ENGLISH TEACHING, CERTIFICATE OF SECONDARY EDUCATION, CONSOLIDATION, ORDINARY LEVEL.

Figures of Speech

Some pupils have great difficulty in understanding and appreciating the metaphorical use of language. This can present problems in their reading. Sometimes they use images instinctively in their writing, but discussion of and practice in figures of speech can encourage them to use them more frequently and more effectively. It is not necessary for pupils to know all the technical names, but there is no harm in using them, and they can be useful when referring to them in writing.

The best and simplest form of figure of speech to start with is the simile which most pupils can grasp easily. After explaining what a simile is and gathering a few examples, a way of giving pupils practice in using them is to ask them to write a poem, each line of which is a simile. Good subjects are monsters, giants, wrestlers, motor-bikes, the sea, witches, the wind. The similes don't have to be too serious or too precise so long as the imagination is set into action. Here is an example of such a poem written by a second year remedial pupil:

The Monster

The Monster was as tall as a skyscraper.
Its claws were sharp as javelins.
Its teeth were long and pointed like spikes.
Its breath was foul as a stink bomb.
Its skin was like a pebble-dash house.
Its tail was like a swaying rope.
Its eyes gleamed like silver milk bottle tops.
Its roar was like a football crowd's.
Its chest was broad as a bench.
Its legs were like oak trees.
It moved slowly through the jungle like a steam-roller.
It ripped its victims like sheets of paper and stuffed them in its mouth
And ended up with indigestion.

MICHAEL SAMUEL

It is natural to move on from similes to metaphors by explaining that metaphors are compressed similes, and that a simile like 'In autumn, the leaves lie on the ground like a carpet' can be expressed as the metaphor 'In autumn, the ground is carpeted with leaves'. An examination of personification follows on easily from there. Again, pupils could be encouraged to write a paragraph or a poem concentrating particularly on using effective metaphors and personification.

It is arguable that these are the only figures of speech that pupils need to know—you may argue that they need not even know these—but there are a number of other common figures of speech worth investigating because they can introduce an element of fun and because they encourage pupils to be more aware of the richness and variety of language and its use. Alliteration, for instance, can be introduced through writing tongue-twisters or alliterative poems; onomatopœia through writing down as many words as possible suggesting sounds or by writing a paragraph where particular emphasis is put on using words suggesting sounds. The pun can be introduced through favourite and perennial childhood jokes. A study of figures of speech such as circumlocution, euphemism, hyperbole and rhetorical questions can lead on to an interesting examination of language as it is used or misused. Irony and paradox are more difficult to explain and grasp, but necessary if language is to be appreciated at any depth. The best method of proceeding is to study some examples—perhaps from current reading or collected from various sources—and to discuss them.

A. Figures of speech are discussed in detail in the following sections of *New English*: NE1, Units 2, 5, 6, and 9; NE2, Unit 1; NE4, Units 8 and 9.

C. See also WRITING POETRY.

Films

Films can be used in English studies as a stimulus (perhaps to start off pupils' own discussion and writing, or as a starting point for thematic work); as a visual account of a novel or story pupils have read, leading to a critical comparison of the two; or as something to be studied critically for its own sake (although a full scale critical and technical approach belongs properly to separate consideration as a subject in its own right such as Film Studies).

There is also value in pupils seeing films of classic literature such as *Great Expectations* or *Oliver Twist* or *Wuthering Heights* as an alternative to reading the works themselves. Some pupils will gain an aesthetic experience from reading the books, but most will find such books beyond their capabilities, and will gain much more from seeing the films. This is an equally valid aesthetic experience though of a different kind, and an enjoyable introduction to the works through filmed versions is vastly preferable to no acquaintance with them at all or to unfruitful attempts to grapple through reading with something that is beyond them. This is perhaps a more realistic (if rather artificial or devious) way in which pupils can make some contact with the heritage of English literature.

Films can be shown in school or visits can be made to cinemas. In either case it can make a stimulating break from routine.

The making of films is something that English teachers could consider. This gives valuable practical experience in script writing, acting, directing, editing, and producing, together with the development of necessary critical judgment. However advice on how to set about this is beyond the scope of this entry.

A. Films are referred to in the following Activities sections of *New English*: NE1, Unit 3; NE2, Unit 9; NE4, Units 5, 8, and 10.

B. The following list of novels and plays that have been filmed may be useful:

Kes	*A Farewell to Arms*
Wuthering Heights	*The Old Man and the Sea*
Jane Eyre	*The Royal Hunt of the Sun*
Oliver Twist	*A Man for All Seasons*
Great Expectations	*A Tale of Two Cities*
Spring and Port Wine	*David Copperfield*
Billy Liar	*Scrooge (A Christmas Carol)*
The Long and the Short and the Tall	*Rebecca.*
	The Great Gatsby
Hobson's Choice	*Catch-22*
Saturday Night and Sunday Morning	*Decline and Fall*
	Sons and Lovers
A Kind of Loving	*Brighton Rock*
The Innocents (The Turn of the Screw)	*The Third Man*
	The Fallen Idol
Far From the Madding Crowd	*Our Man in Havana*
The L-Shaped Room	*A Day in the Life of Ivan Denisovitch*
The Millstone	
This Sporting Life	*Hamlet*
Walkabout	*Romeo and Juliet*
Farenheit 451	*Julius Caesar*
Room at the Top	*Richard III*
Oh What a Lovely War	*Henry V*
The Red Badge of Courage	*The Taming of the Shrew*
Shane	*The Railway Children*
Cry, the Beloved Country	*The Amazing Mr Blunden*
To Kill a Mockingbird	*Swallows and Amazons*
Of Mice and Men	*Black Jack*

A High Wind in Jamaica	*Kidnapped*
Animal Farm	*Treasure Island*
Nineteen Eighty-Four	*The Clockwork Orange*
Moonfleet	*Black Narcissus*
A Hundred and One Dalmatians	*The Bridge on the River Kwai*
A Kid for Two Farthings	*To Sir, With Love*
The Diary of Anne Frank	*A Taste of Honey*
The Loneliness of the Long	*The Winslow Boy*
Distance Runner	*The Caretaker*
Lord of the Flies	*Look Back in Anger*
The Spy Who Came in from the	*The Entertainer*
Cold	*An Inspector Calls*

For further ideas, see:

Film in English Teaching, ed. Roy Knight (Hutchinson)
Film Making in Schools, Douglas Lowndes (Batsford)
Look-Out, Richard Mills and Gordon Taylor (Harrap)

C. See also STIMULUS, VISITS.

Free Writing

Blunted imaginations can sometimes be stimulated by being asked to write about anything that a word or a title or a sound or an object suggests. The word might be 'bread' or 'horses'; the title could be 'A Dark Night' or 'The Lost Dog'; the sound might be a whistle or a slammed door; the object could be a piece of rope or a seashell. The instruction should emphasize that any response or any aspect of the subject is possible and that, for this exercise, spelling and punctuation don't matter. There should be a time limit of fifteen or twenty minutes, and the writing should be undertaken in silence so that a concentrated atmosphere can build up. Afterwards, a number of examples of what has been written can be read out. What often emerges is a remarkable range of different ideas suggested by the same initial stimulus and moments of imaginative insight from pupils who have not always shown this kind of creative response in the past.

This is not an exercise to repeat too often, but it can on occasion provide the something different necessary to renew interest.

B. For a fuller account of this kind of approach, see *Free Writing* by Dora Pym (University of London Press).

C. See also CREATIVE WRITING, STIMULUS.

GCE

See ADVANCED LEVEL, CERTIFICATE OF SECONDARY EDUCATION, EXAMINATIONS, ORDINARY LEVEL.

Grammar

What place should the teaching of grammar have in the work of the English lessons? It can be argued that it is possible to write perfectly coherent and acceptable English without knowing about parts of speech or moods or cases or tenses, and this can be so. But when it comes to correcting work or explaining usage, a knowledge of some grammatical terms is useful. How is it possible to explain that 'between you and me' is the form to be used without some reference to subjective and objective cases? Or to explain that 'we would of' should be 'we would have' without reference to parts of speech? Or to explain that 'to come home' is not a sentence without some reference to what a sentence is? There is no point in saying something is wrong unless you also point out why it is wrong and try to make sure that the logic behind the reason is understood.

One of the difficulties is that so much spadework has to be done, so much background knowledge has to be acquired, before explanations of inaccurate or imprecise writing are possible. Points have to be taken step by step, understanding of particular points has to be practised and tested, and sometimes the difference between a noun or a pronoun is never fully grasped. The amount of time spent on grammar has to be carefully moderated so that it does not become a perpetual grind and so that other important things are not neglected.

Grammar should not be taught for its own sake, although it is possible that some grammatical work can direct attention to words and how they are used, and so lead to an interest in words. For instance, there can be some entertainment in working out how many different parts of speech a word like 'round' or 'fast' can be used as; or in working out the parts of speech in a headline like 'Eisenhower flies back to front'; or in explaining the ambiguity of a statement like 'Filling the tank with petrol, the car was ready for the journey.'

To ignore the teaching of grammar, on the other hand, is as bad as over-emphasizing its importance and practice. To rely on the pupil picking up what he needs from his own reading and writing seems too haphazard a scheme. There must be times when pupils are given information about how words work and how sentences are constructed, and it is better that that information should be given in a systematic and methodical way so that an over-all picture of how English grammar works can be achieved. This means regular lessons on grammar in the earlier years, gradually piecing together a knowledge of how the language works, with the hope that in later years pupils will have sufficient grounding to understand explanations about mistakes and misusage.

New approaches to the teaching of grammar and to the way in which language is organized have become current, but the old Latinate terms and descriptions seem to me to give the clearest view of how the language is constructed and used.

A.   The Language sections of NE1, NE2, and NE3, are very much concerned with grammar, with how the English language is constructed and how it works. For explanations of common solecisms, see NE4, Units 6 and 7.

B.   For other attitudes towards grammar and language, see:
Language and Learning, James Britton (Penguin)
Grammar, Frank Palmer (Penguin)
A Grammar of Modern English, W. H. Mittens (Methuen)
A Modern Approach to English Grammar, James Muir (Batsford)
Language Across the Curriculum, Michael Marland (Heinemann)
Children Using Language, Anthony James and Jeremy Mulford (OUP)
Teaching English: A Linguistic Approach, John Keen (Methuen)
Language in Use, Peter Doughty, John Pearce, and Geoffrey Thornton (Arnold)

C.   See also CLAUSE ANALYSIS.

Group Work

English lessons can be class based or group based; pupils can also work in pairs or individually. Group work can be useful in discussion where a number of groups can discuss the same subject or different aspects of the same subject, reporting their findings back to the class as a whole. If organized in an orderly and sensible way, this kind of arrangement could encourage more pupils, who might be intimidated from speaking in a class discussion, to contribute. The same is true of group work in drama and other activities.

Writing and research can also sometimes be organized in groups.

For instance, with thematic work, each group could be required to produce a folder of writing on the particular theme to include creative writing, factual reports, poems, research, etc., with individual members contributing items. A number of magazines or newspapers could also be produced within a class on a group basis, with either each group devising its own magazine or each concentrating on one particular aspect of the magazine, such as stories, poems, news, sports, opinions, humour, graphics.

Groups can work more effectively if each is arranged in a circle around a table. Each group should have as wide a range of ability within it as possible, unless there is a special reason for having all the weakest together. Alternatively, it might work out satisfactorily for pupils to choose their own groups according to their interests or friends.

The introduction of team teaching for a particular year or for a particular project is another way in which a variety of group structures of pupils can be set up.

A. Many of the drama assignments in *New English* are intended to be undertaken in groups. Much of the discussion suggested could also take part in groups as an alternative to class discussion. The writing assignments are designed for individual use, but there is no reason why, on occasion, groups should not work on the list of assignments or use the list as the basis for building up group folders or group magazines. Group discussion is considered in NE4, Unit 7.

C. See also DRAMA, INDIVIDUAL WORK, MIXED ABILITY, TEAM TEACHING.

Head of Department

The Head of department needs to be a leader and inspirer as well as an organizer and a good teacher. A department is not just the sum of the talents of its individual members; a good head of department can support the weak, encourage the concerned, cajole the lazy, inspire the jaded. The English department should be at the hub of any good school and its influence should spread throughout the school and have an effect on the general atmosphere of the school and on school policy. An energetic, enthusiastic, vital head of department can unify his team so that this is achieved.

On a more mundane level, here are some of the areas of responsibility which the head of an English department has:

He is responsible for the preparation and revision of the syllabus in the light of educational trends and the needs of the school, after consultation with the members of his department.

He should have some share in the development of the curriculum of the school in conjunction with other heads of department and senior staff.

In consultation with the person responsible for the timetable, he should allocate teaching groups to members of his department. The head of department himself should teach right across the ability and age range and should share out teaching groups fairly and effectively to the other members of the department.

He is responsible for organizing regular meetings to discuss the work of the department and formulate its policy. Agendas should be drawn up and minutes published.

He should be aware of the career aspirations of members of his department and should provide advice and training (through delegation and additional responsibilites, etc.).

He is responsible for the checking and supervision of the work done with each class, including the regularity of marking, the setting of homework, and prompt attendance at lessons.

He is responsible for the supervision and guidance of probationary teachers and student teachers in his subject.

He should have the right to advise on the appointment of teachers to his department.

He is responsible for the spending of the department's capitation allowance in consultation with the members of his department and for advising about additional resources and equipment. He is also responsible for the care and effective use of books, equipment and resources.

He is responsible for the general over-sight of the progress of individual pupils in English and for discussing pupils with particular difficulties with pastoral staff.

He is responsible for the preparation of and marking of examination papers and for examination entries.

He is responsible for the effective planning of and preparation for out-of-school visits (e.g. to cinemas, theatres, exhibitions) and of any extra-mural activity (e.g. magazine, school play, discussion group, debating society).

This is a long list of responsibilities, and even so it may not be complete. It gives some idea of the kind of areas where a head of department's influence and effectiveness can be felt. It is worth remembering that the head of an English department is likely to be on a higher salary than that of many heads of junior schools: his responsibilities are also consequently very great.

B. For more detailed advice, see:
Head of Department, Michael Marland (Heinemann)

C. See also DEPARTMENTAL MEETINGS, SYLLABUS.

Handwriting

How much fuss should English teachers make about pupils' handwriting? Probably not too much. By the time pupils have reached the secondary school, their writing style has been largely formed and there is not much to be done about it. And let's be honest—most of the handwriting is perfectly legible. Teachers sometimes overreact to what they consider bad handwriting when their own or that of other adults is illegible: another case, perhaps, of double standards—expecting perfection from pupils when we ourselves are fallible. That is not to say that teachers should not go on demanding and expecting neat work and stressing the importance of clarity in the interests of good communication.

With a few pupils, remedial help may be necessary—going back to basics and using a copying book to relearn how to form the letters and join them together. Other possibilities are to write larger or smaller than usual, write on alternative lines for a while, print instead of write, learn a completely different kind of script such as italic. For an extreme case, a pupil may be encouraged to use a typewriter.

B. A particularly useful book on handwriting is *The Skills of Handwriting* by Reginald C. Phillips (available from R. C. Phillips Ltd., 70 High Street, Oxford). This deals very clearly with the basic principles of manipulation and letter structure and is a book all English teachers will find useful.

Heritage of English Literature

See AIMS OF ENGLISH TEACHING, CHILDREN'S LITERATURE, FILMS, NOVELS, PLAYS, POETRY, SHAKESPEARE, SYLLABUS, TEN ESSENTIAL POEMS.

Homework

The homework policy of the English department may depend on the homework policy of the school. Some people may consider that homework is unnecessary; the reasons for supporting homework are that it encourages a pupil to study and work on his own without having to rely on the help of the teacher or other pupils, and it is an extension of the work done in the classroom, enabling the pupil to cover more ground.

Homework should be interesting and constructive, not just a mechanical chore. Ideally, the pupil should do his homework because he enjoys the work and is interested in it and wants to carry on with it at home. English homework need not just be writing or reading or doing an exercise. It could be watching a particular programme on television, going to the library to get a book on a particular subject or to do some research, collecting information on a topic by asking people questions, finding and cutting out a picture or a newspaper article or an advertisement to take to school.

The amount of homework pupils could be expected to do in English would vary from about half an hour a week in the 1st year to about an hour and a half a week in the 5th year. Pupils studying 'A' Level English should be expected to do about five hours a week on their own.

There is likely to be a resistance to homework on the part of some pupils, and the department should have a clearly laid down policy about what to do in cases like this. One effective method is to organize a departmental private detention after school for pupils who fail to do their homework. If a firm line is taken at the beginning, it is possible to reduce the problem.

The basic question which the English department (and other departments) has to decide is should it force pupils to do homework for their own good, or should pupils be regarded as old enough and mature enough to take responsibility for themselves and their own futures and be allowed to do homework or not as they choose.

Individual Work

Since pupils are of different abilities and work at different rates, much of the work of the English lesson has to be individually based. This refers particularly to reading and writing. Some pupils will read and write more than others, and the teacher must have ideas for further work, resources, and books which he can bring into play for such pupils. This is particularly necessary if the class is a mixed ability one.

A. The instructions for the writing assignments in *New English* say 'Choose several of the following to write about'. The instructions are deliberately left vague like this so that the teacher can amplify them and specify the number of assignments he expects each individual pupil to manage according to his ability.

C. See also GROUP WORK, MIXED ABILITY.

Language

See AIMS OF ENGLISH TEACHING, CERTIFICATE OF SECONDARY EDUCATION, CLAUSE ANALYSIS, CORRECTION OF WORK, DIALECT, EXAMINATIONS, GRAMMAR, ORDINARY LEVEL, PRONUNCIATION, SKILLS, SPELLING, STANDARD ENGLISH, VOCABULARY.

Language Across the Curriculum

The Bullock Report of 1975 highlighted the question of the place of language in teaching—not just the teaching of English, but the teaching of all subjects. While on one hand, the report simply re-enforces the long-held concept that all teachers are teachers of English, it nevertheless brought to attention the following points:

Pupils often concentrate on giving the teacher the answer expected or the 'right' answer rather than using language to express ideas in a way that shows that pupils have really understood the ideas.

Group discussion rather than class discussion allows more pupils to express and formulate their ideas.

Pupils don't have sufficient opportunity to verbalize their ideas and by so doing make the ideas their own.

Too much emphasis is put on written work and not enough on oral work.

Pupils learn the manner of presenting historical or scientific or literary facts rather than expressing these facts in a way that shows genuine understanding.

Too much written work is accepted as a final draft when it should in fact be seen as merely a stage on the way to a final draft and should be modified and revised in the light of further information and thought.

Further research also needs to be considered. For instance, the Schools Council project on 'The Effective Use of Reading' suggests that the books pupils are asked to read are too difficult and contain vocabulary and concepts which are far above their reading ages; that outside English lessons little reading took place which lasted more than a minute at a time; and that often the purpose of the reading was to find the answer to a question rather than to reflect on the whole meaning of the passage.

The findings of the Bullock Report and of other research have repercussions not just for teachers of English but for all teachers. All teachers use language and have a responsibility for seeing that pupils understand its use, therefore it is important that every school has a language policy which all teachers do their utmost to put into effect. The following points could be considered for inclusion in such a policy:

1. As much oral work as possible should be done so that pupils have the opportunity of formulating ideas, opinions, and concepts in their own words.
2. Group discussion rather than class discussion can give pupils the chance to express themselves orally.
3. Specialized vocabulary should be clearly explained and pupils should be given the opportunity to use it in speech and writing so that they can make it their own.
4. Particular attention should be paid to the correction of spelling.
5. Pupils should be encouraged to provide and use their own dictionaries.
6. All kinds of writing—imaginative, report-making, personal, argumentative, factual, letter-writing, etc.,—should be encouraged.
7. Pupils should be encouraged to revise and rewrite work and not to think of the first effort as the final draft.
8. Teachers must ensure that the 'readability' of a text is suitable for the reading ages of the pupils for whom it is intended.
9. Worksheets must be clear and legible and preferably typed or printed.
10. Pupils should have the opportunity to read for sustained periods and for over-all understanding.

B. See:

A Language for Life; The Bullock Report (HMSO)

The Effective use of Reading, eds. Eric Lunzer and Keith Gardner (Heinemann for the Schools Council)

Language Across the Curriculum, Michael Marland (Heinemann)

Language Across the Curriculum, Mike Torbe (Ward Lock)

Letters

Letters may well be the only form of writing many of our pupils will indulge in or be required to do after they leave school. It is therefore worthwhile spending some time on ensuring that pupils know how to set out a letter clearly and coherently. As far as possible, assignments involving the writing of letters should be closely related to real life. Small ads in local or evening newspapers form a good source for real life situations. Writing off for information or material is another area which is valuable as this may even elicit a reply.

A. For an account of how to set out letters and for suggested assignments in letter-writing, see NE4, Unit 7.

C. See also AUDIENCES, WRITING.

Library

Many pupils are intimidated by libraries—both public libraries and school libraries. One pupil described his feelings like this: 'I do not like going to the library for it is too quiet. There are so many books that they seem to get on top of you.' This is the kind of resistance that has to be overcome.

The library must be made attractive with much display material—posters, dust-covers of books, clear instructions on the use of the library, and where to find things. The atmosphere should be welcoming and not prohibitive. Some schools have splendid libraries and the door is kept permanently locked. There is the danger of books being stolen, and safeguards must be taken against this, but at least this proves that pupils appreciate in some way the value of books.

Ensuring that pupils become familiar with the library is a way of overcoming the inhibitions about libraries that many pupils feel. When pupils come into the school, the workings of the library should be clearly explained—how books are arranged on the shelves, how catalogues are organized and how to find a book, the particular scheme the school has for issuing books. If the school has a librarian, so much the better. If not, the English teacher must undertake this task. Library lessons are valuable in helping the familiarization process. Exercises can be set which require pupils to use catalogues and reference books. Research in connection with themes can be undertaken. A silent reading lesson can encourage use of library books. Newspapers and magazines should be available for casual browsing.

The usefulness of the local library with its larger stock of books should also be emphasized to pupils as well as the ease of joining. Research projects and homework assignments could encourage pupils to use the local library. The local library may also have facilities for providing sets of books on loan to the school for a particular project.

The person responsible for stocking the library should keep his eye on reviews in newspapers like *The Times Educational Supplement*. The School Librarian Association's quarterly magazine is another valuable source of current information and reviews.

A. Many of the items in the Activities section of *New English* suggest research which requires the use of the library. The Reading Lists can also provide pupils with titles to look out for when they go to the library.

C. See also CHILDREN'S LITERATURE, CLASS LIBRARIES, MULTI-RACIAL ENGLISH, REFERENCE BOOKS.

Listening

Along with reading, writing and talking, listening is one of the skills which the English teacher has to try to inculcate in his pupils. Perhaps training in listening has always been necessary, but today it seems doubly so. The television in the corner (where chat is possible while a programme is going on) has a lot to answer for. Many people in a theatre audience see nothing wrong in chatting during a performance just as they would if they were at home. The same is true in the classroom. However, if pupils are to learn, then they must be disciplined to listen when listening is required. This is something which the English teacher—and every teacher—must insist upon.

B. See:
The Quality of Listening, ed. Andrew Wilkinson (Macmillan)

C. See also AIMS OF ENGLISH TEACHING, DISCUSSION, SKILLS.

Magazine

There is nothing more revealing about a school than the magazine it produces. Broadly, magazines are of two kinds: the closely-packed, double-columned official ones full of school societies, rugby fixtures and notes on old boys with two or three self-conscious pages of 'creative writing'; and those given over almost entirely to creativity, show-pieces perhaps for the English and art departments, but genuinely allowing individual children's voices to be heard.

Contributions can be invited, though the response will vary. Probably more effective is to collect pieces of work done in the English lessons. In this way, pupils have the encouragement of seeing their work in print and a picture of the kind of work done in English can be shown. Possibly, a particular theme for the magazine could be suggested and most of the contributions could relate to this theme. Collaboration with the art department and the photography department, if there is one, are vital to provide art work in its own right or to encourage pupils to provide illustrations specifically for the writing.

The form of production of the magazine will depend on the resources of the school. A professionally printed volume gives the contents a greater prestige, but the expense may well be prohibitive. If the school has off-set litho equipment, a very stylish magazine can be produced. If not available in school, such facilities may be found at a teachers' centre or a local college of education or university department of education or arts centre. Even ordinary duplicating methods, with the use of electric stencils for the art work, can produce presentable results, and this is certainly preferable to no magazine at all. An editorial staff of pupils should be involved in selecting material and planning the lay-out, though is it probably wise to have some adult supervision or control to make sure that things are organized.

All pupils of the school should be given copies of the magazine rather than having to buy it. In this way, all pupils have the chance of appreciating the work of the pupils who are published and have the chance to see the kind of standards of writing that the English department expects.

As well as the official school magazine, there are opportunities for producing class magazines on a smaller scale. These can arise out of the work of the class and act as motivation, or they could be special projects that are undertaken. For instance, a local campaign run by Help the Aged could lead to a class producing a magazine dealing with old age in a creative and factual way for sale in connection with the campaign.

The extra effort and work that producing a magazine involves are well worth it. It shows that the English department is alive, and it provides an incentive for pupils to have their work published. It is interesting to note too that it is not just the brightest pupils who produce work suitable for inclusion in a school magazine. Often, less able pupils can write a piece that is exciting and deserves commendation, and publishing it in a magazine can give them a boost in morale and help them to make progress.

A. Many of the examples of children's writing in *New English* were originally written as part of English lessons and subsequently published in school magazines. For lists of these items, see the various indexes of the four volumes.

B. For further examples of poetry, see *Children as Poets*, ed. Denys Thompson (Heinemann) which contains a selection of poems written by schoolchildren and published in school magazines.

C. See also COMPENDIUMS, CREATIVE WRITING, WRITING POETRY.

Mixed Ability

Mixed ability is what comprehensive education is about—at least as far as English is concerned. Children of all types should be able to learn about and from each other. The hope is that weaker pupils will benefit from the example of the better work of more academic pupils. There will be examples of excellence for them to strive towards. The greater accuracy and more abstract reasoning ability of brighter pupils may also influence the weaker pupils. But it is not all one sided. The hope is that the more academic pupils will gain something from the generally less inhibited, more imaginative and more vocal less academic pupils. There are a lot of assumptions here, but this represents the kind of benefits mixed ability could provide.

A further advantage of mixed ability grouping is that it prevents the formation of a 'sink' group with no example or incentive for improvement and with all the concomittant problems of behaviour that one would expect when all the pupils of low ability are gathered together. In a mixed ability grouping, pupils of this kind are likely to behave better and to have more chance of receiving individual attention while the rest of the pupils continue with some other work.

A particular justification for teaching English in mixed ability groupings can be seen if we consider imaginative work. When it comes to imaginative work, there is little difference in response between top and bottom stream pupils: both are capable of responding and of producing interesting and exciting work—the only differences are the degree of correctness (though lack of correctness is not necessarily a barrier to communication and the extent to which ideas are thought through and developed).

The use of the thematic approach in English works particularly well with mixed ability groupings. Most pupils, of whatever level, are able to contribute something to oral discussion; all pupils are able to produce something in the way of imaginative writing in response to a stimulus; much of the modern literature used and recommended appeals to all pupils (and the use of the teacher as reader ensures that it can be grasped and enjoyed even by pupils with reading problems). The use of themes also allow pupils to work at different rates and the brighter pupils would be expected to cover more ground and to explore at greater depth.

Teaching a mixed ability group makes greater demands on the teacher. He has to cope with a much wider range of learning (and perhaps behaviour) problems. He has to have a much greater range of material and resources available. He has to be able to organize work so that a large number of independent projects can take place simultaneously. Enthusiasm and vitality are essential. If the teacher does not believe in the validity and rightness of mixed ability teaching, then he is unlikely to be successful at it.

There is no reason why mixed ability teaching should consist solely of a series of worksheets with each individual pupil making his way through the series at his own rate, moving from one sheet to the next—though this is the idea some teachers have of mixed ability teaching. There may be a place for this kind of approach, when pupils are working, for instance, through a series of written assignments in order to build up a file on a particular theme, but it is very far from being the full story.

There should also be opportunities for group work within the mixed ability class. For instance, there should be group discussions with one member of the group acting as secretary to report back to the full class. Research projects could be undertaken in groups. Even reading and writing could be undertaken in groups: a bright pupil reading to the rest of the group or giving an account of a book he has read and reading extracts; a group composition or stories or poems could be attempted, and written work could be corrected and revised by the group.

The composition of the groups is important. Unless there is a very definite reason for it, groups should not be formed and graded according to ability as this defeats the whole purpose of mixed ability teaching. Each group should have within itself a range of ability. Alternatively, pupils should be allowed to form their own groups: it is surprising how genuinely mixed in ability groups chosen in this way are.

Teaching the class as a whole still has a large part to play with the mixed ability class. Stimuli can be presented to the class as a whole. Many points about grammar, vocabulary, and spelling can be discussed with and practised by the whole class. Much reading, if carefully chosen, can be done by the class as a whole. The same is true of much discussion work and drama. One of the values of the mixed ability class is the sharing of experience and the contributions pupils with different backgrounds and abilities can make towards these experiences. Another is the possibility of pupils developing together without some being segregated and having to overcome a sense of failure.

A. *New English* is designed to be used with mixed ability classes. Some pupils will undoubtedly find some sections difficult, but the work is intended to be demanding and is intended to stretch pupils. Teachers using the course will have to help and adapt where required.

B. For further advice and comment on mixed ability teaching, see:
Mixed Ability Groupings, R. Peter Davies (Temple Smith)
Case Studies in Mixed Ability Teaching, ed. A. V. Kelly (Harper and Row)
English in Practice, eds. Geoffrey Summerfield and Stephen Tunnicliffe (CUP)
Teaching English Across the Ability Range, Richard W. Mills (Ward Lock)
Teaching Mixed Ability Groups, ed. E. C. Wragg (David and Charles)
Team Teaching and the Teaching of English, Anthony Adams (Wheaton)

C. See also CHILDREN'S LITERATURE, GROUP WORK, INDIVIDUAL WORK, SYLLABUS, TEAM TEACHING, THEMES.

Multi-Racial English

English teachers must recognize that Britain is a multi-racial society and must take this into account in their teaching and in the material they use. The existence of a multi-racial society is more apparent in some areas than in others, but the need for acceptance and tolerance throughout Britain is vital, whether the particular area you teach in is multi-racial or not. There should be opportunities in English lessons for talking about the different backgrounds from which people come; the books chosen to be read should deal naturally with people from different races or should present situations where there is a clash of cultures (as in *Walkabout* by James Vance Marshall) which provide the chance for discussion. You should make sure that appropriately illustrated textbooks are available, that is, books which show black and white as natural members of our society. Discussions about immigrants may have to deal with some of the problems, but they should not be solely negative: the more positive sides such as the variety and vitality that can result should also be emphasized.

There should be many opportunities for writing. Many of the pupils in our school are now 'second-generation immigrants' and therefore not immigrants at all, but topics such as 'my family', 'the country I should like to visit' or 'my favourite food' can provide the chance for them to write or talk about the countries their families have come from. A responsive attitude on the part of the teacher can then be communicated to the class. Imaginative writing which requires pupils to write from the point of view of someone starting life in a strange country can extend understanding and sympathy. (A poem such as W. H. Auden's 'Refugee Blues' might be a starting point here.) A discussion about some of the facts of immigration could help to dispel some of the myths that may have arisen and should discourage prejudice. (Information may be obtained from the Commission for Racial Equality, Elliot House, 10/12 Allington Street, London SW1E 5EH.)

The important thing is to make sure that 'immigrant' pupils feel that their views and experiences are just as valid and valuable as anyone else's and that they are equal and natural members of the society of the classroom and of society as a whole. In this way self-esteem can be raised and feelings of rejection modified. This will not go all the way to counterbalance the prejudice and discrimination they face in society in general, but at least it is a start, and perhaps as much as the school is able to do on its own.

When it comes to the language spoken by some immigrant children, there are problems. The use of West Indian Creole, for instance, should not be totally discouraged. It should be accepted as a perfectly valid means of communication alongside standard English. Stories (for example by Samuel Selvon) should be read and accepted. Writing in Creole should be permitted and appreciated—though as a separate exercise from the writing of standard English, just as there may be occasions when Scottish pupils might be encouraged to write something in the vernacular of their everyday speech. For examination purposes, children normally have to try to write in as near to standard English as possible, but there is no reason why Creole or any other dialect should not co-exist with standard English in the pupil's world.

With pupils such as Asians or Cypriots learning English as a second language, the case is different. Such things as the omission of articles or the use of the continuous tense instead of the simple past or present have to be corrected and explained.

The library can also play its part by making sure that there are plenty of up-to-date books dealing with the countries of origin of pupils and that old-fashioned history or geography books are removed as well as books with a racist slant. Where possible, newspapers and magazines such as the American *Ebony* should be regularly available.

An increasing number of novels are becoming available which describe life from the point of view of black people and life in a multi-racial society. They should be readily accessible in the library and the classroom. Here are some examples. They vary greatly in the background they describe and in the age-group and ability range they would appeal to, and care is needed in selecting from this list books that would work with particular classes or pupils.

Black Boy, Richard Wright
The Peacock Spring, Rumer Godden
The Basketball Game, Julius Lester
Invisible Man, Ralph Ellison
Cry, the Beloved Country, Alan Paton
To Sir, With Love, E. R. Braithwaite
To Kill a Mockingbird, Harper Lee
The Grass is Singing, Doris Lessing
East End at Your Feet, Farrukh Dhondy
The Contender, Robert Lipsyte
The Experience of Colour, ed. Michael Marland
The Break-In, Barry Pointon
The Friends, Rosa Guy
The Narrow Path, Francis Selormey
Things Fall Apart, Chinua Achebe
A Taste of Honey, Shelagh Delaney
The Jersey Shore, William Mayne
When Rain Clouds Gather, Bessie Head
Mine Boy, Peter Abrahams
The City of Spades, Charles MacInnes
The Lonely Londoners, Samuel Selvon
Moses Ascending, Samuel Selvon
Miguel Street, V. S. Naipaul
A Year in San Fernando, Michael Anthony
The Cay, Theodore Taylor
Old Mali and the Boy, D. R. Sherman
The Evidence of Love, Dan Jacobson
Black and White, ed. John L. Foster
McHiggins the Great, Virginia Hamilton
How Many Miles to Babylon?, Paula Fox
The Slave Dancer, Paula Fox
Native Son, Richard Wright

Marassa and Midnight, Morna Stuart
The Six, Janet Green
The Trouble with Donovan Croft, Bernard Ashley
I, Juan de Pareja, E. B. de Treviño
Roll of Thunder, Hear My Cry, Mildred Taylor
The First of Midnight, Marjorie Darke
The Cloud with a Silver Lining, C. Everard Palmer
My Father Sun-Sun Johnson, C. Everard Palmer
Ways of Sunlight, Samuel Selvon
Another Country, James Baldwin
Blues for Mr Charlie, James Baldwin
Go Tell It on the Mountain, James Baldwin
The Fire Next Time, James Baldwin
Sounder, William H. Armstrong
The Drummer Boy, Cyprian Ekwensi
Nine African Stories, Doris Lessing
Sixty-Five, V. S. Reid
The Siege of Babylon, Farrukh Dhondy
Hackney Half-Term Adventure, Kenneth Worpole and John Boler
Small Accidents, Sabir Bandali
In the Melting Pot, Chelsea Herbert
Equiano's Travels, Paul Edwards
A Wedding Man is Nicer than Cats, Miss, Rachel Scott
Nobody's Family is Going to Change, Louis Fitzhugh
Sophia Scrooby Preserved, Martha Bacon
Black Midas, Jan Carew
Shanta, Marie Thoger
Parveen, Anne Mehdevi
The Young Warriors, V. S. Reid
Joey Tyson, Andrew Salkey
The Games Were Coming, Michael Anthony
Cricket in the Road, Michael Anthony
Second Class Citizens, Buchi Emecheti

Teachers can explore the general area of race and multi-racial education more thoroughly by referring to the following:

Children and Race, David Milner (Penguin)
Racial Disadvantage in Britain, David Smith (Penguin)
The West Indian Experience in British Schools, Raymond Giles (Heinemann)
Teaching in Multi-Racial Schools, David Hill (Methuen)
Between Two Cultures, (Community Relations Commission)
Five Views of Multi-Racial Britain (Commission for Racial Equality)

A. The multi-racial context has been kept very much in mind in *New English*. See the following extracts:

Cricket in the Road, Michael Anthony (NE1, Unit 9)
The Night the Water Came, Clive King (NE1, Unit 6)
The Narrow Path, Francis Selormey (NE1, Unit 7)
Man, in England, You've Just Got to Love Animals, Samuel Selvon
  (NE1, Unit 5)
Sandra Street, Michael Anthony (NE2, Unit 1)
Dogs of Fear, Musa Nagenda (NE2, Unit 8)
The Black Pearl, Scott O'Dell (NE2, Unit 2)
The Boy Who Was Afraid, Armstrong Sperry (NE2, Unit 2)
African Boy, Grace Huxtable (NE3, Unit 2)
Walkabout, James Vance Marshall (NE3, Unit 3)
Black Boy, Richard Wright (NE3, Unit 7; NE4, Unit 5)
The Games Were Coming, Michael Anthony, (NE3, Unit 9)
Table Tennis Champion, (NE3, Unit 9)
36 Children, Herbert Kohl (NE4, Unit 2)
Telephone Conversation, Wole Soyinka (NE4, Unit 5)
The Lady Sings the Blues, Billie Holiday (NE4, Unit 6)
Asian Marriage (NE4, Unit 9)
The Lonely Londoner, Samuel Selvon (NE4, Unit 5)
    Note also: NE4, Unit 5, on Intolerance, where questions about race and prejudice are raised.

B. For further information, see:
Books for the Multi-Racial Classroom (The Library Association)
Race, School and Community (NFER)
    The Commission for Racial Equality publishes useful pamphlets such as *A Guide to Asian Names*, *Education for a Multi-Racial Society* and *Dialect in Schools*. The National Association for Multi-Cultural Education can also provide useful advice.

Music

Music can be an effective stimulus for encouraging an imaginative response in writing. It can be used as part of the material of a particular theme. For instance, there is a wealth of music that could be used for the theme of the sea—Wagner's Overture *The Flying Dutchman*, the Sea Interludes from Benjamin Britten's *Peter Grimes*, the 'Sinbad' episode from Rimsky-Korsakov's *Scheherezade*, Mendelssohn's Overture *The Hebrides*, Hamish MacCunn's Overture *The Land of the Mountain and the Flood*, Arnold Bax's *Tintagel*, Vaughan

Williams's *Sea Symphony*, Debussy's *La Mer*, etc. One or other of these pieces could be used to help elicit descriptive words or phrases or could be played to create a mood which pupils are then asked to write about. The music could be repeated while the pupils write.

Alternatively, music can be used as an isolated stimulus creating an unusual sound or an unusual atmosphere. Pupils can then be asked to write about anything the music suggests to them. Some interesting imaginative work can be produced in this way. Here is a short list of music which has proved effective and which teachers might like to try. Unlike the sea music suggested earlier, it is usually better to use only three or four minutes of one of the following—enough to establish the mood.

Aaron Copland, *Appalachian Spring*
   Rodeo
Debussy, *Prélude à L'Après-midi d'un Faune*
   Nocturnes
Delius, *Brigg Fair*
   On Hearing the First Cuckoo in Spring
Elgar, Introduction and Allegro for Strings
   Cello Concerto
Gluck, 'Dance of the Blessed Spirits' (*Orfeo*)
Holst, *The Planets*
   The Perfect Fool (Ballet Music)
Mussorgsky, *Pictures at an Exhibition*
Poulenc, *Les Biches*
Prokofiev, *The Love of Three Oranges Suite*
   Lieutenant Kije Suite
Ravel, *Daphnis and Chloe*
   Mother Goose Suite
Rimsky-Korsakov, *The Golden Cockerel Suite*
Rodrigo, Guitar Concerto
Sibelius, *Finlandia*
   Symphony No. 2
   Tapiola
Stravinsky, *The Rite of Spring*
Tchaikovsky, *Romeo and Juliet*
   Francesca da Rimini
Michael Tippett, 'Ritual Dances' (*The Midsummer Marriage*)
Vaughan Williams, *Sinfonia Antarctica*
   The Lark Ascending
Vivaldi, *The Four Seasons*

Here is an example of a 4th year pupil responding to the 'Daybreak' section of Ravel's *Daphnis and Chloe*.

71

Fantasy

Harlequins? Columbines? Spirits? No, they are departing.
The dusky dimness of the wind-swept wood envelops,
Encloses them, they disappear, crying, wailing.
The waterfall nearby still tumbles, falls to the valley below.
It is a dream, eyes closed, sleep drifting, drifting on ...
The scene changes—
Silent miles of soft white sand; a dark sky, black, inky;
Impenetrable water; palms blowing.
The wind rises in some nameless unknown part of the air, rushing
Sweeping, tossing—huge waves discard frothing white foam,
Which rolls, halts and is greedily reclaimed by the sea.
Again the thunderous crashing of the cataract as it cascades,
Falls, quietens.
The eastern sky is streaked with gold, pink, silver lights.
A crimson circle rises higher, higher, illuminates the sky.
A distant splashing of a thousand waves,
The fading descent of the waterfall.
The sun is shedding brilliant light everywhere,
Mysterious voices call, their crying increasing—louder, louder.
Then they in turn are beguiled, recalled by the forest.
The dream is ending, fleeing.
Dawn has risen. People awake.

ANNE WHITAKER

Music can, of course, play an important part in drama, in creating a mood, in accompanying or suggesting movement, and in initiating and providing a framework for full-blown dance drama. This is particularly true for drama work with younger pupils. For instance, pieces like Grieg's 'In the Hall of the Mountain King' from *Peer Gynt*, the instrumental version of *West Side Story*, Dukas's *The Sorcerer's Apprentice* or Mussorgsky's *A Night on the Bare Mountain* could be used as the basis for movement exercises out of which develop situations and improvisations. The Grieg piece could be about a meeting of witches in a forest glade with the festivities or rituals becoming more and more frenzied. The music from *West Side Story* could provide the movement and motivation for a basketball game (using a real ball or an imaginary one) developing into a fight between the two teams. And so on.

Here are some further examples of music which could be used in this way:

Malcolm Arnold, *Tam O'Shanter*
  English Dances
  Scottish Dances

Borodin, *In the Steppes of Central Asia*
  Polovtsian Dances
Copland, *El Salon Mexico*
De Falla, *Love the Magician*
Gershwin, *An American in Paris*
Liszt, *Les Preludes*
  Mephisto Waltz
Meyerbeer, *Les Patinuers*
Ravel, *Bolero*
  Pavane for a Dead Infanta
  La Valse
  Introduction and Allegro
Sibelius, *En Saga*
  The Swan of Tuonela
Stravinsky, *The Firebird*
  Petrushka
Walton, *Façade Suite*
All the examples of music quoted are by classical composers. The fact that pupils are more likely to be accustomed to current pop music doesn't invalidate this use of classical music. In fact, it could be an advantage as pupils may listen to it with fresh ears.

A. Suggestions for the use of music will be found in the Activities sections of *New English* as follows:
Fairs and Circuses, NE1, Unit 8
The Sea, NE2, Unit 2
Ghosts, NE2, Unit 4
Winter, NE2, Unit 5
Machines, NE2, Unit 7
Men and Beasts, NE2, Unit 8
Hunting and Hunted, NE3, Unit 5

C. See also DRAMA, PICTURES, POP MUSIC, STIMULUS, WRITING POETRY.

Newspapers

These can be a valuable source of resource and critical material. They can provide articles to relate to current events or themes being studied or as starting points for discussion or writing. They can provide pictures to use as the stimulus for writing or for display purposes relating to a theme. The amount of space devoted to different aspects (e.g. news, sport, entertainment, comment, advertisement) by different newspapers can be studied. Comparisons can be made of the treatment of the same news item by different newspapers. Advertisements can be used as the basis for letter writing or as an exercise in criticism. The local newspaper can be used to provide motivation for a letter to the editor on some controversial issue. Pupils can be encouraged to write up an event as though for publication in a newspaper, imitating the relevant style and using headlines. The critical analysis of a newspaper article, distinguishing between news and comment, fact and half-truth, sweeping generalization and bias, is also valuable, since newspapers are likely to be almost the sole reading material of many pupils when they leave school

Another way of achieving an understanding of how newspapers work is to ask pupils to make up their own newspapers. News items such as 'Tiger Escapes' or 'Fire Sweeps Through Factory' or 'School Broken Into' could be invited. Pupils could 'mock up' their own front pages. As a different kind of comprehension exercise, pupils could be asked to retell a poem like Wilfred Gibson's 'Flannan Isle' or a novel like Golding's *Lord of the Flies* as a newspaper report.

A.   Extracts from newspapers are used in *New English* as follows:
The Guardian, NE2, Unit 6
The Evening Standard, NE2, Unit 6
The Sunday Times, NE3, Unit 5
The Observer Magazine, NE3, Unit 8
The Radio Times, NE3, Unit 8
The Sunday Times, NE3, Unit 8
The Stage, NE3, Unit 8
The Sunday Times, NE4, Unit 3
The Radio Times, NE4, Unit 5
The Guardian, NE4, Unit 6
The Guardian, NE4, Unit 9
The Observer Magazine, NE4, Unit 10
The Sunday Times, NE4, Unit 11

B.   See:
Newspaper Writing, Lionel Birch (Harrap)

C.   See also ACTIVITIES, ADVERTISEMENTS, DISPLAY.

Novels

Some of the arguments for asking pupils to read novels are given in the entry on CHILDREN'S LITERATURE—the providing of vicarious and aesthetic experience, the extension of critical faculties, the encouragement of reading for pleasure and entertainment. But as pupils become older, it is more difficult to find novels that can be recommended and that can be studied in depth. It is hard to think of adult novels published later than *Lord of the Flies* or *Room at the Top* or *The Loneliness of the Long-Distance Runner* which are suitable for adolescents and which are within their range of experience. More recent novelists seem to be concerned with areas that are more explicitly adult in tone or deal with them in a style which makes it difficult for young readers to approach them or makes them not worth approaching. Novels like Malcolm Bradbury's *The History Man* or Paul Scott's *The Raj Quartet* or John Fowles's *The French Lieutenant's Woman*, to mention but three, for all their merits, are not suitable for use as teaching material in the classroom. Possibly, the growing range of novels for 'young adults' (such as *The Flambards Trilogy* by K. M. Peyton or *The Siege of Babylon* by Farrukh Dhondy or *The Outsiders* by S. E. Hinton) will be more accessible and more appropriate. The teacher is therefore thrown back on the 'standards' of the 1950s and 1960s or on 'classics' which may still retain some validity in the classroom (such as *Great Expectations* or *Silas Marner* or *Robinson Crusoe*).

Here are some 'adult' novels which may appeal to pupils in the 3rd, 4th, and 5th years as class readers or as library books:

William Golding, *Lord of the Flies*
George Orwell, *Animal Farm*
   Nineteen Eighty-Four
Barry Hines, *A Kestrel for a Knave*
Alan Sillitoe, *The Loneliness of the Long-Distance Runner*
   Saturday Night and Sunday Morning
Stan Barstow, *A Kind of Loving*
   Joby
John Braine, *Room at the Top*
Ernest Hemingway, *The Old Man and the Sea*
John Wyndham, *The Day of the Triffids*
   The Chrysalids
Anthony Burgess, *The Clockwork Orange*
David Storey, *The Sporting Life*
Evelyn Waugh, *The Loved One*
John Steinbeck, *The Pearl*
   Of Mice and Men
   The Red Pony
Nevil Shute, *Pied Piper*
Jack Schaefer, *Shane*

Wolf Mankowitz, *A Kid for Two Farthings*
Rumer Godden, *Black Narcissus*
Pierre Boulle, *Bridge on the River Kwai*
Harper Lee, *To Kill a Mocking Bird*
E. R. Braithwaite, *To Sir, With Love*
Alexander Solzhenitsyn, *One Day in the Life of Ivan Denisovitch*
Keith Waterhouse, *Billy Liar*
    There is a Happy Land
Laurie Lee, *Cider with Rosie*
John le Carré, *The Spy Who Came in from the Cold*
J. D. Salinger, *The Catcher in the Rye*
D. R. Sherman, *Old Mali and the Boy*
Richard Wright, *Black Boy*
Lynne Reid Banks, *The L-Shaped Room*
Edna O'Brien, *Girl with Green Eyes*
Paul Gallico, *The Snow Goose*
    A Small Miracle
Alan Paton, *Cry, the Beloved Country*
Samuel Selvon, *The Lonely Londoners*
    Here are some novels for 'young adults' which could be worth considering:
James Vance Marshall, *Walkabout*
Robert C. O'Brien, *Z for Zachariah*
Joan Lingard, *Into Exile*
    Across the Barricades
Josephine Kamm, *Young Mother*
    Out of Step
Paul Zindel, *The Pigman*
John Christopher, *The Guardians*
Hester Burton, *The Rebel*
Penelope Farmer, *Charlotte Sometimes*
Glendon Swarthout, *Bless the Beasts and Children*
Farrukh Dhondy, *East End at your Feet*
    The Siege of Babylon
K. M. Peyton, *Pennington's Seventeenth Summer*
    The Beethoven Medal
    Pennington's Heir
    The Flambards Trilogy
Julius Lester, *The Basketball Game*
John Rowe Townsend, *The Intruder*
Rumer Godden, *The Peacock Spring*
Alan Garner, *The Owl Service*
Christopher Leach, *A Temporary Open Air Life*

Robert Lipsyte, *The Contender*
Joan Tate, *Sam and Me*
Beverly Cleary, *Fifteen*
S. E. Hinton, *The Outsiders*
  That Was Then This is Now
Martin Ballard, *Dockie*
John Christopher, *Dom and Va*
Ivan Southall, *Josh*
Jane Gardam, *A Long Way from Verona*
John Branfield, *Nancecuke*
  The Sugar Mouse
Honor Arundel, *The Longest Weekend*
Robert Westall, *The Machine Gunners*
Marjorie Darke, *The First of Midnight*

The length of the novel can sometimes present problems when it comes to a critical approach. There is the problem of getting pupils to read it for a start (and, if the novel is a short one, it may be a case of the teacher reading it to the class). But there is also the problem of being able to see the novel as a whole. Much discussion about theme and plot, construction and pace, characters and background is necessary if pupils are to be weaned away from simply giving an outline of the plot and assuming that they are giving a critical account. It is worth persevering as it is through reading and responding to what they have read that pupils are able to extend their experience.

Although it would not replace the reading and study of novels, it is worth considering the use of the short story as an occasional alternative to or as leading up to the study of the novel. Because of its length, it is possible to discuss the short story critically with a class and for pupils to be able to write about it in a constructive and analytical way.

A. Many extracts from novels are used in the Reading and Understanding and Writing sections of *New English*. The Reading Lists suggest titles that pupils and teachers could explore. Advice on critical writing about the novel is given in NE4, Unit 9.

B. For further information, see:
The Reluctant Reader, Aidan Chambers (Pergamon)
Choosing Books for Children, Peter Hollindale (Elek)
Introducing Books to Children, Aidan Chambers (Heinemann)
Reading Together, Kenyon Calthrop (Heinemann)
Children and their Books, Schools Council Research Studies (Macmillan)

Reluctant to Read?, ed. John Foster (Ward Lock)
For series which cater specifically for the adolescent reader as opposed to the young reader, see:
Topliners (Macmillan)
Pyramid Books (Heinemann)
Peacock Books (Penguin)
Books for New Adults (Bodley Head)

C. See also CHILDREN'S LITERATURE, CLASS READERS, SHORT STORIES.

Oral Work

In the course of English work, every pupil should be encouraged to take part in the full range of oral work. Being able to express oneself confidently and fluently in speech is one of the most important elements of English training. The range of activities is wide: answering questions, taking part in discussions and debates, giving instructions and explanations, giving a prepared talk, speaking on a subject from notes or without preparation, giving a demonstration, reading aloud with or without preparation, introducing a poem or an extract which is read aloud, giving an account of a piece of research, taking part in various drama activities. There should be opportunities for formal and informal oral work. Fuller accounts of these activities are given under other entries.

A. Many opportunities are provided in *New English* for oral work of different kinds. Advice on preparing for the oral part of the CSE examination is given in NE4, Unit 5.

C. See also ACTIVITIES, DEBATES, DISCUSSION, DRAMA, GROUP WORK, READING ALOUD, SCHOOL PLAYS, SKILLS, SPEECHES, SPOUT, TAPE RECORDING.

Ordinary Level

The most significant and surprising fact about 'O' Level GCE in English is that there are two examinations and two awards. 'O' Level English Language and 'O' Level English Literature are entirely separate. Considering the belief which many English teachers hold that English language and literature are indivisible, and that it is impossible to teach one without the other (or that the best method is to teach one through the other), this separation is rather strange. No appreciation of literature is required of an 'O' Level English language candidate (other than what is incidental to a comprehension exercise), and it is possible for him to gain a pass without having read a novel or a poem. Not that 'O' Level English Literature is necessarily much better: it is possible for a candidate to gain a pass after reading only three books. These limitations raise doubts about the whole foundation on which GCE syllabuses and examinations are based—although, to be fair, it could be argued that they leave the teacher with more freedom to organize what will be taught in the classroom.

The 'O' Level English language examination consists basically of a composition, a comprehension exercise and possibly a summary or a letter or an exercise in correcting badly expressed writing. There are variations from one examining board to another. Some examining boards now use a multiple-choice comprehension exercise. While the subjects proposed for composition were once dry and limited, they are now more varied and interestingly presented—pictures are often used as a stimulus. The passages set for comprehension also tend now to be much more carefully chosen to be within the range of experience of candidates.

With some boards, spoken English is a kind of extra qualification. This involves reading a text aloud and discussing it and other topics with the examiner. This is not a compulsory part of the examination, and so there is the rather anomalous situation whereby for French 'O' Level and other modern languages oral ability is required whereas for English it is assumed or taken for granted.

For 'O' Level English literature, three prescribed texts are required to be studied in detail—a play (invariably by Shakespeare), a selection of poetry and a novel. The choice of texts often leaves much to be desired, and they tend to be pedestrian, unadventurous, and remote from the experience of pupils. Alternative syllabuses requiring pupils to have a less detailed knowledge of six or eight texts are also set. This provides the opportunity for more choice, but may not allow for the practice in close study of a text which is necessary for pupils who are going on to study 'A' Level English literature.

With the teaching of 'O' Level English language and English literature, it is difficult to avoid the examination grind. Some practice in examination techniques, in planning essays, in looking at past papers, in writing specimen answers is required. English language can be enlivened by choosing subjects in which pupils are interested and to which they can respond, and it is possible to find time to read and discuss books not directly related to the examination. With English literature it is not so easy to avoid following the syllabus closely. Time is one limiting factor as the full year is probably necessary simply to get through the texts with the appropriate amount of explanation and discussion. There is little opportunity for additional background reading or looking at texts which are more likely to appeal to the tastes and experiences of pupils. Much depends on the enthusiasm and vitality of the individual teacher. We all know of plays or poems which have been ruined through the drudgery of having to swot them up for an examination. Perhaps there is a case for saying that for many of our pupils an examination in English literature is unlikely to be an inspiring or expanding experience; nor is it likely to teach them much about appreciating or understanding literature.

Those teachers who find the prescribed texts for 'O' Level English Literature uninspiring or who want to take a more active part in determining the kind of examination their pupils are being prepared for should explore the alternatives that are available. For instance, some examining boards (such as Oxford and Cambridge) allow a school to devise a large part of its 'O' Level literature syllabus. In one such scheme, paper two consists of nine units of continuously assessed work (on novels, plays, and poems chosen by the school) which counts for 60 per cent of the total mark with the other 40 per cent being allocated to either a short story or a literary study written at the end of the year. The continuously assessed work is marked internally; the short story or literary essay is moderated externally. The process of devising such courses can be exciting and can keep teachers interested in their examination texts since they have chosen them.

A. *New English* is designed as a basic English course which could lead to CSE or 'O' Level. NE4 mainly follows the CSE approach but would also be beneficial for pupils sitting 'O' Level English language. For sections specifically referring to 'O' Level, see Units 1 and 11. See *NEC* for material more directly and fully related to studying for 'O' Level.

C. See also ADVANCED LEVEL, CERTIFICATE OF SECONDARY EDUCATION, EXAMINATIONS.

Personal Growth
See AIMS OF ENGLISH TEACHING, CREATIVE WRITING, DRAMA.

Personal Writing

Some of the most interesting and articulate writing that pupils can do is when they write about their own experiences, and there should be many opportunities for doing this in the course of their English work. Areas such as family life, hobbies, friendships, after-school and weekend activities, holidays, home areas, part-time jobs can all give rise to lively writing. Not all pupils will be ready to write truthfully and openly about their own experience or about their family background, so care must be taken to allow the possibility of their writing being real or imaginary. The teacher's response to personal writing needs to be sensitive and sympathetic: pupils are unlikely to write about their own lives if they find that the teacher makes fun of what they have written or if they find that some of the things they write about become common knowledge in the staff room.

A. There are many suggestions for personal writing in each unit of *New English*. The following themes particularly lend themselves to this kind of response:

All About Me (NE1, Unit 1)
At School (NE1, Unit 2)
Christmas (NE1, Unit 4)
Pets (NE1, Unit 5)
Holidays (NE1, Unit 9)
Down My Way (NE2, Unit 1)
Fireworks and Bonfires (NE2, Unit 3)
The Senses (NE2, Unit 9)
Family Life (NE3, Unit 1)
Food and Drink (NE3, Unit 3)
Being Ill (NE3, Unit 4)
Getting Into Trouble (NE3, Unit 6)
Parents (NE4, Unit 1)
Love and Marriage (NE4, Unit 9)
Now and Tomorrow (NE4, Unit 10)

A large number of examples of personal writing by pupils is used in *New English*. For details, see the Index of Authors and Titles of each volume.

B. For further examples of personal writing, see:
Children as Writers (Heinemann)
Enjoying Writing, ed. A. B. Clegg (Hart-Davis)

C. See also CORRECTION OF WRITING, CREATIVE WRITING, WRITING.

Pictures

Visual material has a valuable place in English teaching. A well-chosen picture (of a city scene, for instance, or a stormy sea) can be the basis for a discussion, particularly with younger pupils. The discussion could centre on the situation depicted or on ideas arising out of the situation. It could be used to stir the imagination and to extend vocabulary by eliciting words and phrases that could describe the scene. These ideas could later be used in writing.

As a more direct stimulus for writing, pupils can be given pictures on which to base a description or a story. Some pupils are likely to be more interested in visual appeal than in words or abstract ideas, and the use of a picture as the starting point for a story might well set their imaginations going more productively. The picture can also help them with filling out the details of their story: it is there; it can be referred to. Pupils can be asked to find their own pictures to write about, or the teacher can build up a collection cut from newspapers and magazines and pasted on board. These could be related to a theme or individual pictures dramatic enough to be likely to elicit a response. Another source of visual material can be found in postcard reproductions of paintings. These can often produce impressive results where pupils are asked to write a poem, and both 'old master' reproductions and modern abstract paintings can be effective. Here is an example of a poem inspired by a painting of the corn harvest by Brueghel:

Twelve noon of an August day.
The wives come laden with bread, cheese and cider
For their hard-working husbands
Who turn their heads to the may-tree and wearily retrace their foot-
    steps.
They sing, and as they stumble through the sea of corn they raise
    startled
Partridges—lost for a home.
They collapse at the feet of their wives and eat.
The older ones don't eat yet, they struggle on,
And as the field of gold shrinks and turns to brown
Tiny rabbits with irregular gait bounce towards a wood.
Behind them in the distance
A still silent sea of corn crowns a hill.
A wagon of hay is left in the shade while the old mare
Crops cool grass and clover.
Still further back another field—scythes laid at rest

To spare the living square a few more moments.
In the valley too villagers have stopped.
Everywhere there is quiet, the singing ceased.
But still the elders swing and cut.

MARTIN LONGMAN

Most examining boards, both at 'O' Level and CSE, now usually include one or more picture which candidates can choose as the basis for their writing. It is therefore important that pupils should have had the experience of doing this in the past.

Another use for visual material is when displaying pupils' work. Pieces of writing on a particular theme can be put up on the wall and illustrated by relevant pictures. The finding of suitable pictures could be one of the assignments given to the class as part of their work.

A. Most units in *New English* include one or more illustrations designed to start off a discussion or to act as the basis for writing. For instance, in Unit 1 of NE1, two illustrations of schools in the 1890's are offered to encourage pupils to make comparisons with today; the illustrations of weird inventions by Heath Robinson in Unit 7 of NE2 are there to inspire pupils to create their own machines; Hokasai's Wave in Unit 2 of NE2 could be used to evoke words and phrases describing the sea. The use of pictures like these is intended also to ensure that less able pupils can make their contribution to the general work on a particular theme, and certainly in this area they should be able to feel that they are working on equal terms with other pupils.

Pictures are included as a part of the CSE examination given in NE4, Unit 11.

B. Some published material is available for those teachers who find it difficult to collect their own pictures. See:
Pictures for Writing, Michael Marland (Blackie)
More Pictures for Writing, Michael Marland (Blackie)
See also:
Poetrycards, C. Copeman and D. Self (Macmillan)
Perspectives: A Visual Approach to Creative Expression, Barry Walters (Wheaton)

C. See also ANTHOLOGIES, DISPLAY, MUSIC, STIMULUS, WRITING POETRY.

Plays

Simply reading a play is no substitute for seeing it in performance, but with comparatively few opportunities for young people to see plays that are suitable in the theatre, there is really no alternative. Even if likely to be a literary rather than a dramatic experience, reading a play can have its value. Plays sometimes deal with people and themes in a more straightforward and immediate way than other mediums and can extend pupils' awareness of these areas. They also provide the opportunity for analysis, interpretation and criticism.

Rehearsing and producing a play in the classroom is impracticable other than in exceptional circumstances. There really seems to be no other approach than for the play to be read silently or for parts to be allocated and for the play to be read round the class. The 'actors' could have the chance of preparing their parts. Much will inevitably be lost through inexpert reading, but it is surprising how much pupils are able to grasp even in a halting and undramatic version. With some plays it may be possible to use a recorded performance. One way of providing some dramatic context would be to improvise on the theme of the play or on a situation in the play.

The same problem exists with plays as exists with novels: there was a sudden eruption of plays in the 1950s and 1960s by Wesker, Arden, Delaney, Osborne, and Bolt, for instance, which it is perfectly possible to use in the classroom, but more recent writing has been such as to make translation to the classroom very difficult. More recent plays by young writers tend to be unsuitable because of their language, their subject matter, or their experimental approach which makes them unsatisfactory as read texts.

There are few plays of much value to use with younger secondary school pupils, but the following could be considered for use with older pupils:

A Taste of Honey, Shelagh Delaney
The Long and the Short and the Tall, Willis Hall
Hobson's Choice, Harold Brighouse
An Inspector Calls, J. B. Priestley
When We Are Married, J. B. Priestley
Serjeant Musgrave's Dance, John Arden
The Widowing of Mrs Holroyd, D. H. Lawrence
The Murder of Maria Marten or The Red Barn, Constance Cox
All My Sons, Arthur Miller
The Crucible, Arthur Miller
Saved, Edward Bond
The Royal Hunt of the Sun, Peter Shaffer

St Joan, G. B. Shaw
Arms and the Man, G. B. Shaw
The Winslow Boy, Terence Rattigan
The Matchmaker, Thornton Wilder
Roots, Arnold Wesker
A Man for All Seasons, Robert Bolt
Journey's End, R. C. Sherriff
The Kitchen, Arnold Wesker
The Caretaker, Harold Pinter
Spring and Port Wine, Bill Naughton
The Glass Menagerie, Tennessee Williams
The Corn is Green, Emlyn Williams
Under Milk Wood, Dylan Thomas

A. How to write critically about plays is discussed in NE4, Unit 10.

There are also extracts from the following plays:
The Miracle Worker, William Gibson (NE2, Unit 9)
Julian, Ray Jenkins (NE3, Unit 6)
The Winslow Boy, Terence Rattigan (NE3, Unit 6)
Five Green Bottles, Ray Jenkins (NE4, Unit 1)
Serjeant Musgrave's Dance, John Arden (NE4, Unit 8)
A Taste of Honey, Shelagh Delaney (NE4, Unit 9)

B. Published series of plays worth exploring are:
Hereford Plays (Heinemann)
Dramascripts (Macmillan)

C. See also DRAMA, SHAKESPEARE, VISITS.

Poetry

Often pupils will come from the junior school never having read any poetry, and many teachers dislike poetry or feel diffident about using it in class. This is a pity because poetry can often provide invaluable material for lessons and is an essential part of English studies. It can work at so many levels—entertainment, stimulating ideas, studying the skill of using words, extending experience, providing literary experience.

Part of the trouble in the past has been the fact that poetry has been presented as a separate and special item for study with a poetry lesson every week devoted to it. It is not surprising in these circumstances that teachers have found it difficult to teach and pupils have been turned off by it. Far better is to use poetry whenever relevant to the other work of the English lessons. A poem can act as the stimulus for writing or as the starting point for a theme; it can be used to balance or contrast with the ideas, emotions, or attitudes of another piece of writing; a group of poems can illustrate different approaches to an experience or different ways of using language. A poem can also, of course, be read as an experience in its own right.

One complaint which pupils frequently hold against poetry is the tendency for poems to be used as comprehension exercises and for them to be analysed to death. Some examination and study of the language and meaning of the poem will doubtless be necessary, but a poem should be primarily a literary experience not a vocabulary or comprehension test.

Choosing the right poems is vital. They should not be such that barriers of language, style, convention, or experience are raised. This does not mean that the poems chosen need be simple or banal. The intensity contained in a good poem is such that if it is well presented by the teacher pupils can often appreciate an experience which may in other circumstances be considered too difficult for them. Twentieth-century poetry is likely to be more readily assimilated and enjoyed than eighteenth- or nineteenth-century classics. Poems by poets such as the following are likely to interest pupils: Thomas Hardy, Dylan Thomas, Edward Thomas, W. H. Auden, Siegfried Sassoon, Wilfred Owen, R. S. Thomas, Ted Hughes, Philip Larkin, Charles Causley, D. H. Lawrence, Robert Frost, Tony Connor, Seamus Heaney, Vernon Scannell, John Betjeman, Brian Patten.

The poems used need not always be by established poets. Often in the small magazines or weekly newspapers poems appear which can have a particular relevance. Teachers should be on the look-out for poems like these, and should build up their own stock of poems which they know can work in the classroom. Above all, if teachers are to succeed in convincing pupils that poetry is worth looking at and studying, then they must themselves have a genuine interest in poetry and maintain an interest in current trends in poetry.

If a school is extremely fortunate, it may have the opportunity of having a poet in residence under the Arts Council scheme. More realistically, it is possible to invite poets to the school to read their poems and talk about poetry under the 'Writers in Schools' scheme. Either way, it could result in a renewed or increased interest in poetry in the school.

A. A large number of poems are used in the course of *New English*. See the indexes of the various volumes.

B. The following books could be useful:
Where's That Poem?, Helen Morris (Basil Blackwell)
Teaching Poetry, James Reeves (Heinemann)
Presenting Poetry, ed. Thomas Blackburn (Methuen)
Poetry in the Making, Ted Hughes (Faber)
A Guide to Teaching Poetry, Eric Newton and Graham Handley
(University of London Press)

C. See also ADVANCED LEVEL, AIMS OF ENGLISH TEACHING, ANTHO-
LOGIES, CERTIFICATE OF SECONDARY EDUCATION, COMIC VERSE, MUSIC,
ORDINARY LEVEL, PICTURES, TEN ESSENTIAL POEMS, WRITING POETRY.

Pop Music

There is a place for 'pop music' (or whatever the current term may
be) in the English classroom, but a very limited one. Since it is a
main interest with many pupils, it should be discussed and some
degree of criticism and discrimination should be encouraged. The
words of some pop songs (by the Beatles or Bob Dylan, for instance)
are readily available and deserve to be looked at. But teachers are
in the business of raising standards, and bland acceptance of the
culture of pop music does nothing to achieve that.

A. See NE4, Unit 1, for the words of 'She's Leaving Home' by
Paul McCartney and John Lennon.

B. See:
Popular Music and the Teacher, Keith Swanwick (Pergamon).

C. See also MUSIC.

Precis

See SUMMARY.

Project Work

It can be useful, perhaps once a year, for pupils to undertake an
extended piece of work. So much of the writing we ask pupils to
do requires a comparatively short period of concentration that the

occasional longer span can be rewarding and productive. The kind of project could be the writing of a novel or play; a survey of some literary form such as science fiction or spy stories or a particular author; an illustrated account of a hobby or interest such as football, motor cars, pop music, fishing or fashion; a series of stories about the same characters or on a particular theme such as war or crime or love; an extended essay on television or advertising or scientific discovery or sport.

The danger with some of these subjects is that they can deteriorate into a list of football teams and players, for instance, or into a list of pop stars and their records. The impetus can also weaken and interest flag if the project is stretched out over too long a period. The teacher has to balance the value of allowing the pupil the opportunity of writing about something he is keen on against the size of the literary content of the project. With those projects where creative writing is a much more obvious element, such as writing a novel or a series of stories, much careful guidance will have to be given about theme and characters, about organizing different episodes and developing situations. Perhaps a quest or journey novel like Tolkien's *The Hobbit* or Anne Holm's *I Am David* or Ian Serraillier's *The Silver Sword* could be used as a model here, or Mark Twain's *The Adventures of Tom Sawyer* or the stories about Tommy Mac by Margaret Stuart Barry.

Pronunciation

Pronunciation becomes a relevant concern of the teacher of English only in so far as it raises barriers to communication. He must stress the importance of speaking clearly and intelligibly—enunciation perhaps rather than pronunciation. It is a matter of social courtesy to speak in such a way as not to put a strain on the listener. There should be no attempt to iron out dialectal burrs except where these are so thick that they prevent understanding. Disputatious areas such as the pronunciation of words like 'harass', 'controversy', 'schedule', or the alternative stress on words like 'research', 'content', 'object', and 'suspect' could be commented on.

B. See:
Accent, Dialect and the School, Peter Trudgill (Arnold)

C. See also
DIALECT, STANDARD ENGLISH.

Punctuation

If what their pupils write is to be understood, teachers somehow have to get across to those pupils the importance of punctuation. It is not an easy task. Correcting and discussing written work with individual pupils is one approach. Class lessons on the use of the full stop, the comma, quotation marks is another. Exercises can include pupils correcting each other's work, passages to be rewritten correctly punctuated (perhaps using actual examples by pupils), dictation, examples of ambiguity caused by weak punctuation to be corrected. Whether there is any carry-over from exercises to improved written work is open to doubt. Often, pupils can punctuate accurately in exercises and then go back to their old ways in their own work. It remains a problem where perseverence and patience are necessary, and where a united effort by all teachers (not just English teachers) is required.

There can sometimes be a conflict between encouraging pupils to write imaginatively and with pleasure and helping them to improve the technical aspects of their writing. Quantity and quality are important, but pupils can be inhibited if what they have written with enthusiasm is returned covered in red corrections. Perhaps pupils could be asked to write in rough in the first instance without worrying too much about punctuation, and then to revise it and rewrite it, but this process is not one that pupils generally find attractive. An alternative is to ask for imaginative but inaccurate work which has been corrected by the teacher to be copied out so that it can be displayed on the classroom wall. The pupil can see a positive side to this kind of repetition.

A. Much stress is laid on the rules of punctuation and on punctuation exercises in *New English*. See particularly NE1, Units 3, 4, 6, 8, and 9; NE2, Units 2, 3, 7, and 8; NE3, Unit 2; NE4, Units 1 and 2.

B. For further information and exercises, see:
Practical Punctuation, Ian Gordon (Heinemann)

C. See also CORRECTION OF WORK, LANGUAGE ACROSS THE CURRICULUM, REPAIR WORK, SENTENCES.

Pupil Power

One of the most important resources in English teaching is often ignored or neglected, and that is the pupil. What the pupil has to contribute to the English lessons in terms of experience is enormous; by bringing out and allowing that experience to be shared, the teacher can find many directions in which to follow it up and build it into the work of the class. Much of this experience will emerge in talk about families, friends, the area pupils live in, hobbies and interests, encounters with the police and shopkeepers and neighbours, part-time jobs, holidays, schoolteachers, youth clubs. Apart from the way in which it is allowed to emerge in talk and discussion, this experience can be channelled by asking pupils to give prepared talks to the class about things they are interested in, and, by sharing, they thus extend the experience of others.

Pupils probably know more about some subjects, such as football, the police, youth clubs, fishing, discos, motor cars, chess, than their teachers. And it is not just the obvious subjects that crop up. Every class has its expert or enthusiast in some way-out area which might go unnoticed if an opportunity is not there for sharing it and which could provide stimulating material for a lesson. An example of the kind of thing that could happen is given in the chapter in Barry Hines' *A Kestrel for a Knave* in which Billy Casper talks about training a kestrel—it should be compulsory reading for all English teachers.

Pupils can even take over the lessons by being asked to give talks like these, by choosing poems or extracts from books to read to the class, by recommending reading to other pupils, by introducing and leading discussions, by reporting back on research or preparing recordings, by chairing and organizing debates. It can also be salutary for the teacher to have to sit at a desk at the back of the room and be reminded of what it is like to be a pupil.

Another way in which pupil power can be harnessed is to ask pupils to bring in material which can be used in lessons. This can range from appropriate pictures and newspaper cuttings, family photographs, poems and extracts, advertisements, objects to write about (such as leaves or bones or fabric), records, or pets or bicycles or stamp-collections which may be used to illustrate individual talks or as things to discuss and write about.

A. There are many opportunities in the oral work suggested in *New English* for pupil power of this kind to be tapped. The Activities sections indicate other areas where it could be harnessed.

C. See also DEBATES, DISCUSSION, DISPLAY, RESOURCES, SPEECHES, SPOUT.

Radio

Radio programmes can provide a valuable source of material to record and use in the classroom. This can range from performances of plays the class is reading to programmes such as Alistair Cooke's *Letter from America* which offer well presented but easily understood thoughts about the world around us for pupils to consider and discuss. Extracts from *Any Questions?* or *Any Answers?* or *Woman's Hour* can similarly form the starting point for discussion. Comedy programmes can be used for entertainment but also as the basis for an analysis of comic technique and for critical comparison. Dramatizations of classics or story-readings can also be useful. There are too the programmes specially produced for schools which often present interesting and stimulating material and for which printed booklets are available so that pupils can follow the text as it is read. The *Radio Times* should be ordered each week by the English department and programmes of particular interest should be displayed and pointed out on a notice-board for pupils to see.

Pupils could also be encouraged to produce their own programmes for the radio medium through the use of tape or cassette recorders. These could be plays or sketches or their own versions of actual programmes. A daily magazine programme could even be broadcast every lunch hour throughout the school if there is sufficient enthusiasm and expertise.

A. Ray Jenkins' short plays *Five Green Bottles* and *Julian*, extracts from which appear in NE4, Unit 1, and NE3, Unit 6, were originally written for radio.

B. The most famous play written for radio is, of course, Dylan Thomas' *Under Milk Wood*.

C. See also TAPE RECORDING, TELEVISION.

Reading

See CHILDREN'S LITERATURE, CLASS LIBRARIES, CLASS READERS, LIBRARY, NOVELS, PLAYS, POETRY, READING ALOUD, READING LISTS, SILENT READING.

Reading Aloud

One of the most valuable experiences pupils have in their junior schools is being read aloud to by their teachers. It has always seemed a pity that this practice of reading aloud to pupils tends to die out in the secondary school. Given a skilled teacher who is able to read aloud effectively with the right amount of dramatic emphasis (not too much!), literature can come alive for many pupils in a way that it can't for them on the written page. This is particularly true with mixed ability classes where some of the pupils will gain greater understanding from the teacher's voice than from stumblingly following printed words. (Some brighter pupils may well prefer to read ahead on their own, and this is fair enough. I have never found that their concentration has been affected by the teacher reading aloud to the rest of the class; and if they finish before the others they can always go on and read something else.)

Reading aloud by the teacher should not be restricted to the odd short story or newspaper article. Complete novels can be read and enjoyed in this way—if the teacher's vocal cords have the necessary stamina. The best way to do this is to read the novel solidly to the class every period for two or three weeks rather than just one period a week. In this way the impetus can be maintained. Even with more senior pupils in the 5th year, especially with CSE pupils, reading aloud by the teacher remains a pleasure and an aid to understanding and appreciation. Some novels, of course, read aloud better than others because of length or style. Here are some that work particularly well:

Dragonslayer, Rosemary Sutcliff
The Tower by the Sea, Meindert DeJong
The House of Sixty Fathers, Meindert DeJong
The White Mountains, John Christopher
I Am David, Anne Holm
The Silver Sword, Ian Serraillier
Smith, Leon Garfield
Animal Farm, George Orwell
Of Mice and Men, John Steinbeck
The Loneliness of the Long-Distance Runner, Alan Sillitoe
Billy Liar, Keith Waterhouse
A Kestrel for a Knave, Barry Hines

It is assumed that pupils will have the books in front of them and will follow the words as the teacher reads, though some pupils seem to gain greater pleasure and understanding from watching the reader.

Not all books are suitable for reading aloud *in toto*. They may be too long, or their remoteness of language or style may present problems. But even here, an edited prepared version could be successful where the teacher has worked out the important and exciting episodes to read aloud and links them by summarizing what happens in between. A full version of *A Christmas Carol* or *Pride and Prejudice* or *The History of Mr Polly* may be too much for a mixed ability class, whereas an edited version on these lines could prove acceptable.

It is difficult to say how often the teacher should stop in reading aloud to explain words or to elucidate plot or character or to check up, through questioning, whether the pupils are following the story or not. My own feeling is that this should be kept to a minimum. The meanings of less common words can be explained in a parenthesis by the teacher as he reads. Discussion points about character and plot and testing that the pupils are still with you can be done at the end of chapters or main episodes. The dangers to avoid are reducing the reading aloud to a vocabulary or comprehension exercise and breaking up the story so much with questioning that the excitement of the narrative is lost.

When the subject 'reading aloud' is mentioned, we tend to think of pupils reading aloud round the class. Is this really a valuable exercise? Children can hardly be expected to have the reading skill of a trained teacher, and a faltering undramatic reading by pupils is likely to kill much of the impetus and drama of a story. Nor is it fair, particularly in a mixed ability class, to expect a pupil who finds reading difficult to read aloud to his peers. Pupils are often eager to volunteer to read aloud (and not always those who are best able to do so) and it may seem a shame to dampen their enthusiasm. Perhaps they could have the opportunity of reading aloud from factual non-dramatic work.

Objections to pupils reading aloud are less valid when it comes to pupils reading their own work. Where a pupil has produced a good piece of writing, it is a valuable form of encouragement to ask him to read it to the rest of the class. It also indicates to the class the kind of standards the teacher is setting and is an incentive to the other pupils to attain this standard. Even here, though, some pupils can be shy or hesitant. The pupil's willingness must always be obtained first, and he should be given the choice of reading himself or having the teacher read.

There still remain, however, the problems of finding out how well pupils can read and of improving their reading skills. A fair way of doing this is to treat it as a separate exercise, unconnected with the excitement of finding out what happens next in their class reader. Pupils can be asked to prepare a particular section of a novel (possibly the same section for all pupils) to read aloud, and comparisons and criticisms made of the effectiveness of different readings.

93

(Clearly, only a few pupils would be heard at a time, or else the repetition of the same extract could become tiresome.) Pupils can be asked to choose and prepare a passage or a poem to read aloud, perhaps on a particular theme. A good reader could be given an opportunity to prepare and read a passage which is coming up in a future lesson. A pupil who is less fluent could have practice in reading aloud by reading quietly to the teacher while the rest of the class is engaged on silent reading or some other task. The important thing is to avoid a situation where a pupil is forced into the embarrassment of revealing his deficiency in reading skill in front of his peers: such a situation could well put him off reading for life.

A. Extracts from particularly recommended novels appear in *New English* as follows:
The White Mountains, John Christopher (NE1, Unit 3)
The Tower by the Sea, Meindert DeJong (NE1, Unit 7)
A Christmas Carol, Charles Dickens (NE1, Unit 4)
A Kestrel for a Knave, Barry Hines (NE1, Unit 5; NE4, Units 2 and 7)
I Am David, Anne Holm (NE2, Unit 9)
Dragonslayer, Rosemary Sutcliff (NE1, Unit 3)
 It is envisaged that most of the extracts from novels and other sources used in *New English* will be read aloud to the class by the teacher so that pupils with less ability in particular will have a greater chance of appreciation and understanding.

C. See also CHILDREN'S LITERATURE, CLASS READERS, MIXED ABILITY, NOVELS, PLAYS, SILENT READING, SPOUT.

Reading Lists

Where possible and appropriate, give reading lists to pupils so that they can extend their experience and continue their interest in a particular area. It might be a list of good westerns or good detective novels or science fiction or books about animals. It is likely that most pupils will ignore such lists and not be interested in having them, but some pupils do use the school library and public library, and some pupils do like to carry on reading on their own. To them, guidance of this kind may be welcome. After all, much teaching is based on pious hope. Because much of our advice falls on stony ground is no reason to stop giving advice: if one or two benefit it will have been worthwhile.

A.   Each unit of *New English* contains a reading list of further books (mainly novels) related to the particular theme of the unit. Pupils can be encouraged to try to get copies from the library and read them so that they can gain further experience of the theme—and also pleasure in reading. The books recommended vary considerably in scope; some require greater stamina and maturity than others. The teacher's advice may be necessary about which books are likely to appeal to individual pupils.

C.   See also CLASS LIBRARY, LIBRARY, SILENT READING.

Reference Books

Pupils should be encouraged to use reference books. The dictionary is obviously the most important reference book that pupils can be referred to, but there are many others which can arouse curiosity and answer queries—such as *Brewer's Dictionary of Phrase and Fable, Everyman's Classical Dictionary, Roget's Thesaurus, Fowler's Dictionary of Idioms*. Reference books like these are usually kept in the library, but having a selection at hand in the classroom can prove very useful. Unusual idioms or references can be checked on straightaway; they can be used as the basis for exercises; they can be stimulating for casual browsing. The use of reference books in this way appeals to the 'let's have a quiz' kind of attitude which many pupils have, and it is one way of arousing an interest in words and how they are used.

A.   Many of the exercises in the Vocabulary sections of *New English* could involve the use of reference books.

B.   Here are some examples of reference books it would be useful to have in the classroom:
Social Trends (HMSO)
Name into Word, Eric Partridge (Secker and Warburg)
A Dictionary of Abbreviations, Eric Partridge (Allen and Unwin)
English Pronouncing Dictionary (Everyman's Reference Library)
The Oxford Dictionary of English Proverbs
Origins: A Short Etymological Dictionary of Modern English, Eric Partridge (Routledge and Kegan Paul)
To Coin a Phrase: A Dictionary of Origins, Edwin Radford (Hutchinson)
The Oxford Dictionary of English Etymology
Concise Etymological Dictionary of Modern English, Ernest Weekly (Secker and Warburg)

A World Treasury of Proverbs (Cassell)
A Concise Dictionary of English Idioms, William Freeman (EUP)
A Book of English Idioms, V. H. Collins (Longman)
A Second Book of English Idioms, V. H. Collins (Longman)
A Third Book of English Idioms, V. H. Collins (Longman)
Dictionary of Idioms, W. S. Fowler (Nelson)
Oxford Dictionary of Current Idiomatic English, Cowie and Mackin (OUP)
Crabb's English Synonyms (Routledge and Kegan Paul)
Roget's Thesaurus
Webster's New Dictionary of Synonyms
Walker's Rhyming Dictionary of the English Language (Routledge and Kegan Paul)
Dictionary of Clichés, Eric Partridge (Routledge and Kegan Paul)
A Dictionary of Slang and Unconventional English, Eric Partridge (Routledge and Kegan Paul)
Usage and Abusage, Eric Partridge (Hamish Hamilton)
Cassell's New French Dictionary
Cassell's Latin Dictionary
A Dictionary of Foreign Words and Phrases in Current English, A. J. Bliss (Routledge and Kegan Paul)
A Reader's Guide to Literary Terms, Beckson and Ganz (Thames and Hudson)
A Dictionary of Literary Terms, J. A. Cudden (Andre Deutsch)
The Best English, G. H. Vallins (Andre Deutsch)
Better English, G. H. Vallins (Andre Deutsch)
English Dialects, G. L. Brook (Andre Deutsch)
Spelling, G. H. Vallins (Andre Deutsch)
The Words We Use, J. A. Sheard (Andre Deutsch)
The English Language, Ernest Weekley (Andre Deutsch)
Etymology, A. S. C. Ross (Andre Deutsch)
The Oxford Dictionary of Quotations
The International Thesaurus of Quotations (Allen and Unwin)
The Penguin Dictionary of Modern Quotations
The Oxford Companion to English Literature
Longman's Companion to Twentieth-Century Literature
Pear's Cyclopaedia
The Faber Book of Epigrams and Epitaphs, ed. Geoffrey Grigson (Faber)
Everyman's Classical Dictionary
The Oxford Classical Dictionary
The Oxford Dictionary of English Place Names
The Oxford Dictionary of English Christian Names

A Dictionary of British Surnames, P. H. Reaney (Routledge and Kegan Paul)
Nicknames, Vernon Noble (Hamish Hamilton)
A Dictionary of Nicknames, Julian Franklyn (Hamish Hamilton)
The Names of Towns and Cities in Britain (Batsford)
English Place Names, Kenneth Cameron (Batsford)
Payton's Proper Names, Geoffrey Payton (Warne)
Brewer's Dictionary of Phrase and Fable (Cassell)
English Language Reference Book, Rhodri Jones (Blackie)

Obviously, it would not be practicable to have all these books available in the classroom, but they do indicate the range that could provide invaluable material. They form a much under-used resource for English teaching. If only a limited number could be available, then they should include a number of assorted dictionaries, a dictionary providing information on etymology, *Roget's Thesaurus*, a dictionary of idioms, a dictionary of classical references, and Brewer's *Dictionary of Phrase and Fable*.

C. See also DICTIONARY, SPELLING, VOCABULARY.

Reluctant Readers
See CHILDREN'S LITERATURE, CLASS READERS, NOVELS.

Remedial English
A full and detailed account of the philosophy and practice of remedial English teaching is not within the scope of this volume. There are so many factors which need to be considered: the infinite patience and tact of the teacher; the necessity of having a calm, unruffled secure personality; the use of games and flash cards and tape recorders and other resources; the need for material which is simple but whose subject matter is relevant to the age-group of the pupils concerned; the teaching of reading; the need for encouragement and support; distinguishing between pupils with learning problems and pupils who have behaviour problems; the use of diagnostic tests and assessment tests. This is an area where the English department needs specialist help from teachers trained in remedial education.

A pupil with a reading age of nine and above ought to be able to cope in a mixed ability class, though clearly a reading age of nine is not very high and he may need some extra help. The form this should take is something the English department should consider.

Should there be a remedial teacher in the classroom with the English teacher? Should the pupil be withdrawn from some lessons to have individual tuition? Should pupils with low reading ages be in a separate class and have most of their lessons together in this separate class? Is the need for extra English or an alternative kind of English?

B. See:

Remedial Education, John McCreesh and Austen Maher (Ward Lock)

Remedial Education, ed. Paul Widlake (Longman)

Reading: Problems and Practices, ed. Jessie F. Reid (Ward Lock)

The Teaching of Reading, Donald Moyle (Ward Lock)

Language, Learning and Remedial Teaching, Roger Gurney (Arnold)

The Slow Learner in the Secondary School, ed. Clive Jones-Davies (Ward Lock)

Some of the series of remedial reading books are worth considering for use with weaker pupils in mixed ability classes, to have in the library, or for use with reluctant readers. They vary in quality and difficulty, but the following are worth looking at:

Inner Ring Books (Benn)

Joan Tate Books (Heinemann)

Club 75 (Macmillan)

Booster Books (Heinemann)

Checkers (Evans)

Knockouts (Longman)

Tempo Books (Longman)

Focus Books (Blackie)

Stories for Today (Heinemann)

C. See also ASSESSMENT, MIXED ABILITY.

Repair Work

Once the foundations of grammar, spelling, and punctuation rules have been laid down, and in spite of the fact that they will need constant repetition, much of the work of improving an individual pupil's technical ability to write English will be in the nature of repair work—pointing out particular words that he spells wrongly, punctuation or stylistic lapses, inelegance of presentation. The pupil can be directed to explanations of the faults in reference books or on worksheets and to specific exercises designed to give practice in getting it right. In an ideal world, written work should be discussed with the pupil as it is being marked. Often, pointing out that there is a mistake in a particular line is enough to enable the pupil to see it and correct it. But matters are not necessarily ideal, and much work has to be marked and returned without oral comment, with the hope that pupils will be conscientious enough to study the corrections and learn from them. It is possible to insist that all mistakes be written out correctly after each piece of writing. Individual teachers will have to make up their own minds whether this is effective in preventing the recurrence of the mistakes, whether the chore of chasing pupils up to make sure they are doing it is worth the effort, and whether this mechanical exercise takes away from the enthusiasm and excitement they are trying to encourage to make the pupil want to express his ideas in writing.

A. Throughout *New English*, pupils are encouraged to keep a spelling and a vocabulary notebook to help them with their own particular problems.

B. Pupils could be referred to the following books to check up on points they may have got wrong:
English Language Reference Book, Rhodri Jones (Blackie)
A Spelling Dictionary, Michael West (Longman)
Practical Punctuation, Ian Gordon (Heinemann)

C. See also CORRECTION OF WORK, PUNCTUATION, REFERENCE BOOKS, SPELLING.

Research

An activity which can enliven English lessons is research—asking pupils to find out about certain topics and bring back the results of their research to share with the rest of the class. It may involve asking parents about leisure activities or schooling when they were young. It may consist of looking in newspapers for accounts of bad weather or accidents or crimes. It may involve going to the local library or the school library to find out about punishments and prisons in previous times or about disasters at sea or about life in other countries. The material can be written up as a report or recorded on a cassette recorder or related orally to the class and can act as the starting point for a discussion or as additional material to extend the study of a particular theme.

A number of important elements connected with the appropriate presentation of research material can be taught and encouraged— such things as how to acknowledge sources, how to present a bibliography, how to lay out a report, how to prepare an interview and introduce a speaker, how to tie in visual material with the text, how to prepare an index, etc.

A.   Many of the items in the Activities sections of *New English* indicate suitable areas for research in the style of those suggested above.

C.   See also ACTIVITIES, LIBRARY.

Resources

The English teacher does not rely solely on chalk and talk. He has to have other resources at hand to provide material for discussion and writing and to supplement his own ingenuity. Books are the obvious prime resource which the English teacher has available, and care has to be taken to see that the right books are secured for the department and that they are readily available when required. There should be reference books, for the use of the teacher and for pupils to use. Worksheets and cyclostyled material are another way of making sure that the right poem or extract is on hand at the right time. Magazines, newspapers, travel brochures, advertising hand-outs, and posters can provide another source of material in the way of articles and illustrative matter which can be useful in teaching. Pupils can be asked to bring in material of this nature where appropriate. The school library should be well stocked with the kind of book the English teacher is likely to need or to which he is likely to refer pupils for private reading or research. The public library too can be used as a source of material, and some libraries are happy to provide collections of books on particular subjects if requested. Records of appropriate music, poetry readings, and plays should also be available as well as tapes of radio programmes. It is too much to expect an English department to have its own films, but the local film library, if there is one, and the commercial distributors should certainly be used. Catalogues for these should be available as well as the catalogues of all the educational publishers.

In order to make use of all this material, the English teacher must have access to a large range of equipment including some kind of printing or duplicating equipment, record players, tape recorders, cassette recorders, cameras, over-head projectors, slide projectors, film projectors, radios, and televisions.

C.   See also LIBRARY, REFERENCE BOOKS, SPECIALIST ROOMS, STOCK ROOM.

School Bookshop

One way of encouraging the idea among pupils that books are things to buy and own and enjoy is to operate a school bookshop. Arrangements can be made with a local bookseller or a specialist firm to purchase books to sell direct to pupils in the school. Actually having the books there for pupils to look at and handle acts as powerful advocacy, especially for pupils who may come from homes where there are no books or for whom there is no convenient bookshop in the area. In addition, the teacher is there to give advice.

Organization is important—choosing the right books, having sufficient storage space, finding the right venue within the school. Publicity and displays of posters and dust-covers can stimulate interest. There could be a second-hand section with items donated by staff where pupils could exchange books. Opening on parents' evenings or open days can also be a good idea so that pupils can persuade their parents to buy.

A. Reading Lists in *New English* indicate some of the titles that may be suitable for the school bookshop.

C. See also CHILDREN'S LITERATURE, NOVELS, PLAYS, POETRY, SHORT STORIES.

School Play

The idea of the school play is often sneered at. Educational drama and improvisation are held to be vastly superior and vastly more rewarding in terms of the personal growth of students. This may well be so, but it does not invalidate the more old-fashioned concept of the school play. As an extra-mural activity, it can provide a stimulating experience for a large number of people. It can result in a new kind of relationship and a new kind of understanding between teachers and pupils. It can enable some pupils who might not otherwise achieve success to have the opportunity to shine and allow them a chance to prove themselves in public and acquire confidence. It can show parents what the school is capable of and act as an incentive to unite the school in common purpose. These are important considerations which should not be devalued.

That having been said, the school play today constitutes something of a problem. Pupils are less ready to stay behind after school or to turn up on a Saturday morning for rehearsal. The idea of doing an annual Shakespeare play or Gilbert and Sullivan opera is less acceptable or possible. So what is the alternative? Four considerations have to be taken into account. The play chosen has to have some value as a dramatic and aesthetic experience and has to be worth doing. It has to involve a large number of people. It has to be of interest to the young people whose time is being taken up. It has to appeal to an audience of pupils, parents, teachers, and friends. This immediately limits the number of plays which are suitable.

A dedicated producer may still be able to enthuse his cast and audience through *A Man for All Seasons* or *The Italian Straw Hat* or *She Stoops to Conquer*, but the days of this kind of production are probably numbered given today's attitudes and climate. Probably what are more workable are one-act plays by Harold Pinter or David Campton in workshop productions, anthology-type presentations of verse, prose, and song on a given theme selected by a particular drama group (on the lines of *The Hollow Crown*), productions which have evolved from classroom or drama club improvisations, or collaborations with the music department such as *Joseph and the Amazing Technicolor Dreamcoat* or *West Side Story* or *Oliver*. These don't necessarily match the aspirations of the old school play concept, but they at least allow for the involvement of young people in a dramatic and public experience.

B. For those teachers who may still wish to try to put on a school play in the traditional way, the following very miscellaneous list of possible plays may be of interest:

A Man for All Seasons, Robert Bolt
The Matchmaker, Thornton Wilder
An Italian Straw Hat, Eugene Labiche
Oedipus Rex, Sophocles
The Dumb Waiter, Harold Pinter
The Bald Prima Donna, Eugene Ionesco
A Servant for Two Masters, Goldoni
She Stoops to Conquer, Oliver Goldsmith
Listen to the Wind, Vivian Ellis
Roots, Arnold Wesker
Androcles and the Lion, G. B. Shaw
St Joan, G. B. Shaw
The Long and the Short and the Tall, Willis Hall
The Trojan Women, Euripides
Zigger-Zagger, Peter Terson
The Thwarting of Baron Bolligrew, Willis Hall
Hobson's Choice, Harold Brighouse
A Penny for a Song, John Whiting

C. See also DRAMA, PLAYS.

Senses

One way of encouraging pupils to improve the quality of their writing is to ensure that they are awake to the effect of any experience they are writing about on the senses and translate this into words. The senses of touch, sight, smell, hearing, and taste should constantly be appealed to so as to find out what they can tell us about the object or situation being written about and so that this object or situation can become a more immediate and real experience to the reader.

Some specific exercises in terms of the senses can help here. For instance, writing down lists of words which have an onomatopoeic effect (such as 'cackle', 'tinkle', 'sizzle') or words for movement which suggest a very definite physical action (such as 'stumble', 'stagger', 'stomp') or words which distinguish between different ways of speaking (such as 'murmur', 'roar', 'stutter'). A list of the different kinds of sounds to be found in a town or in the countryside could be worked into a poem. Similarly the different tastes of foods, the varying textures of wood, wool, silk, and metal, or a series of pleasant or unpleasant smells could be organized into a poem. Ask pupils to look at specific objects and describe them as precisely as possible, particularly in terms of how they appear to the senses. Objects worth trying are a polythene bag, a pendulum, a piece of polystyrene, a balloon, a dahlia tuber, a potato, a bone. It is possible also to play a number of games directing attention to the senses: a pupil can be blindfolded and asked to distinguish between objects by taste (vinegar and salt water), by smell (cheese and paraffin), or by touch (plastic and metal), the aim being to describe the different objects in words rather than by name.

By alerting the senses in this way, it is hoped that pupils will search for words to describe these sensuous experiences more effectively. Instead of writing down the first words that come to mind, they will look for words which recreate in the reader's mind more vivid impressions of what they are writing about.

103

A. Unit 8 of NE3 is specifically concerned with the senses and with stimulating pupils to use words which evoke a response in the reader's mind.

B. For poems dealing with touch, smell, taste, sight, and hearing, see *Five Senses* (Preludes), ed. Rhodri Jones (Heinemann).

C. See also CREATIVE WRITING, STIMULUS, VOCABULARY, WRITING, WRITING POETRY.

Sentences

Writing in sentences is one of the things many pupils find very difficult to do. Nevertheless, it is something that teachers must try to get across, as it is an essential skill if pupils are to be able to communicate in writing clearly, coherently, and literately. Explanations of what constitutes a sentence will be necessary. Practice in writing sentences as separate units (for instance, writing ten sentences about a particular subject; asking pupils in specific pieces of work to take a new line every time they write a new sentence) and in rewriting incorrectly punctuated passages may be of some help. Insisting that pupils write answers to comprehension questions and speak in complete sentences is another way of keeping the ideal of the sentence before pupils' eyes. Pointing out incomplete or 'excessively long' sentences in the pupils' own writing and correcting them may have results. Practice in looking at sentences and examining how they are constructed, including breaking them up into clauses, is another way of directing attention to the problem.

Some of these approaches may seem pedantic, but what is the alternative? Can the teacher really leave the pupil to his own devices and assume that he will automatically learn how to write in sentences? Certainly, the first step is to encourage the pupil to write and to want to write, but there must come a point where, if he is not using full stops or writing effectively constructed sentences, this must be brought to his attention and steps taken to try to remedy the situation. As in many areas of English teaching, a balance has to be maintained between encouragement and criticism. A possible way out of the dilemma would be to specify that particular pieces of writing (perhaps those less creative in nature) would be marked very accurately in terms of sentence structure and that in these pieces pupils should pay especial attention to writing in sentences. There may then be some carry-over to other writing and less chance of inhibiting the imagination and the desire to write.

A. The sentence is a frequently recurring theme in *New English*. For sections dealing specifically with it, see:
NE1, Units 3 and 9;
NE2, Units 4, 5, and 7;
NE3, Units 2, 3, 4, 5, 6, 7, and 8;
NE4, Unit 1.

C. See also CLAUSES, CORRECTION OF WORK, GRAMMAR, PUNCTUATION, REPAIR WORK.

Shakespeare

What is the place of Shakespeare in schools today? The reading of one of his plays presents great linguistic and literary problems if attempted with a mixed ability class. Even listening to a recording with the text in front of pupils is still likely to present a difficult task and it is uncertain how much genuine pleasure or comprehension could be achieved. An actual performance of a play in a theatre may produce a better result if there is preparation and discussion. Even a filmed version of a play may provide a satisfactory alternative.

The study of a play by Shakespeare is required for 'O' Level English literature and 'A' Level English, though whether this is the way to arouse interest in and appreciation of the greatest English writer may be open to question. A top stream selected class in the 4th or 5th year should be able to approach a play by Shakespeare with some degree of understanding and pleasure if it can be put over with verve and enthusiasm, but too often it is simply a case of plodding through the text. Some pupils' interest may be aroused by things peripheral to Shakespearean studies like the Elizabethan stage or the use of music or the supernatural.

It is a difficult dilemma. Many people have been put off Shakespeare for life by having to study a play in school or for an examination; but on the other hand, if Shakespeare is not introduced in school, what chances are there that people will come to him later in life?

B. The following may be worth considering as ways of introducing Shakespeare to today's pupils:
Shakespeare for Secondary Schools, ed. Richard V. Taylor (Macmillan)
The Group Approach to Shakespeare, David Adland (Longman)

Into Shakespeare, Richard Adams and Gerald Gould (Ward Lock)
Tragical-Comical-Historical-Pastoral, ed. Lionel Gough (Arnold)

C. See also ADVANCED LEVEL, ORDINARY LEVEL, PLAYS.

Short Stories

The short story is attractive as a source of reading and critical material. It is usually possible to read it in a lesson, and it is short enough for pupils to discuss it critically and to be able to grasp and analyse the theme and plot, the characters and setting, and the implications behind the story, when they may not have the stamina to study a novel. It can also act as a useful stepping off point and as an example for pupils when they come to write their own stories. Some authors whose short stories pupils should find approachable are: Saki, Katherine Mansfield, D. H. Lawrence, Arnold Bennett, H. G. Wells, James Thurber, Samuel Selvon, Michael Anthony, Doris Lessing, Ernest Hemingway, Scott Fitzgerald, Alan Sillitoe, Stan Barstow, Bill Naughton, Sid Chaplin, O. Henry, Somerset Maugham, John Steinbeck, Muriel Spark, H. E. Bates, Graham Greene, Ray Bradbury, Frank O'Connor, Liam O'Flaherty, Thomas Hardy, Roald Dahl, E. M. Forster.

When pupils come to write their own stories, some guidance is useful. For instance, they should be made aware that exciting or violent action (such as murder or espionage or international crime) is not necessary in a story, and that writing based on personal experience can usually be fresher and more interesting. The influence of television here is very strong and has to be combated. Discussion about structure and characters, about beginnings and endings, about use of dialogue (some pupils tend to write whole stories in dialogue much of which is banal and irrelevant) and use of interesting and evocative words and images is valuable. Much of this guidance can be general and much can come in the form of a helpful comment by the teacher when marking the story. Reading out good stories written by pupils, displaying them on the wall or reproducing them in magazines can also indicate standards and encourage the others.

A. Most of the prose passages in *New English* are extracts from novels or from newspapers, but it was felt important to include some complete short stories. They can be found as follows:
Cricket in the Road, Michael Anthony (NE1, Unit 9)
Man, in England, You've Just Got to Love Animals, Samuel Selvon
  (NE1, Unit 5)

A Snapshot of Rex, James Thurber (NE1, Unit 5)
Sandra Street, Michael Anthony (NE2, Unit 1)
The Old Man at the Bridge, Ernest Hemingway (NE4, Unit 8)
The Pedestrian, Ray Bradbury (NE4, Unit 10)
   For short stories and personal writing by schoolchildren, see
My First Day at School (NE1, Unit 2)
Oh so nearly ... (NE3, Unit 1)
Late Night Coffee Stall (NE3, Unit 7)
Alone (NE3, Unit 7)
A Mother's Fondness (NE4, Unit 1)
Thief (NE4, Unit 6)
Carnations and Cornflakes (NE4, Unit 7)
The Quarrel (NE4, Unit 9)
The Unmarried Mother (NE4, Unit 9)
   Advice on writing short stories is given in NE4, Unit 1. Unit 10
of NE4 includes advice on writing about short stories.

B.   Some anthologies of short stories that may be useful are:
Short Stories of Our Time, ed. Douglas R. Barnes (Harrap)
The Storytellers, ed. Roger Mansfield (Schofield and Sims)
Storyhouse, eds. David Jackson and Dennis Pepper (OUP)
First Choice, ed. Michael Marland (Longman)
A Likely Story, ed. Alan Lynskey (Longman)
Spectrum, eds. Bruce Bennett, Peter Cowan and John Hay (Long-
   man)
Storylines, ed. A. Thompson (Hodder and Stoughton)
Moments of Truth, ed. Frank Whitehead (Hart Davis)
Story, eds. David Jackson and Dennis Pepper (Penguin)
Heinemann Short Stories 1–5, ed. Rhodri Jones (Heinemann)
Imagine, eds. Robert Protherough, John Smith and Leslie Stratta
   (Harrap) is an anthology of short stories written by school-
   children.
See also:
Imprint Books (Longman)
The Heritage of Literature Series (Longman)
The Pegasus Library (Harrap)
The Short Story Series (Murray)

C.   See also NOVELS, WRITING.

Silent Reading

Occasional or regular sessions of silent reading are valuable. They
foster the reading habit and encourage concentration and the ability

to read at length with self-reliance and comprehension. Indeed, for many pupils, these may be the only times in their lives when they will read undisturbed for long periods. For the teacher, sessions like these provide an opportunity to get on with other work, such as catching up on marking, going over written work with individual pupils, explaining points to a pupil who has missed something by being absent, hearing individual pupils read aloud quietly. It might sometimes be felt that a silent reading period is an easy option for the teacher, but it is of value in itself to the pupils, it enables the teacher to do other important work, and it requires effort on the teacher's part to see that it is properly organized.

Class readers could be read silently—though there are problems here about pupils reading at different rates. If the teacher is lucky enough to be able to use the library, pupils could read library books and change them as required. Alternatively, a class library could be set up—a collection of suitable books in a cupboard or a box. A wide range of books would be necessary to cover the great range of interests and abilities in a mixed ability class, and pupils would need guidance in seeing that they choose books that they are likely to enjoy and that they can cope with.

Is a follow-up necessary? How can you tell whether books have been read with pleasure and understanding? A common method is to expect a written book review on completion of each book. As an occasional exercise, this can be useful, with pupils given advice on the kinds of things to comment on and with the development of some kind of critical approach, but there is a danger of this becoming a mechanical chore if it is always the end-product of reading a book, and in the long run it may be counter-productive. Possibly expecting each pupil to keep a list of books read with brief comments and recommendations might be less onerous and more encouraging. At various times pupils could have the opportunity to talk about the books they have read—nothing is likely to make a pupil read a book more than a recommendation from one of his peers. Or silent reading could be seen as being of value in itself with no need of a follow-up. After all, the atmosphere in a classroom or a library where pupils are reading books is enough in itself to tell you whether the books chosen are appropriate and whether the pupils are enjoying and understanding them. This hushed absorbed atmosphere also probably does more for the cause of reading than any amount of exhortation from the teacher or writing about books by the pupils.

A. Reading Lists at the end of each unit in *New English* provide examples of books which pupils could read during silent reading periods and could form the basis of class libraries or be an aid to pupils asked to go to the school or public library to choose a suitable book. Care has to be taken to advise individual pupils on the books which would be appropriate for their tastes and abilities. For instance, the Reading List of 'Family Life', Unit 1, of NE3, contains a wide variety of suggestions. Some of these could be recommended to all, for instance *Smith* (Leon Garfield), *A Dog So Small* (Philippa Pearce), *The Silver Sword* (Ian Serraillier). Others would appeal particularly to girls, for instance *Magnolia Buildings* (Elizabeth Stucley), *Carrie's War* (Nina Bawden). Some could be recommended only to the more mature or more literate, for instance *Blowfish Live in the Sea* (Paula Fox), *David Copperfield* (Charles Dickens), *The Diary of a Nobody* (George and Weedon Grossmith), and such readers might find titles like *The House of Sixty Fathers* (Meindert DeJong), *The Children Who Live in a Barn* (Eleanor Graham) and *Gumble's Yard* (John Rowe Towsend) too juvenile for them. In order to use these Reading Lists effectively, the teacher therefore has to have a wide knowledge of children's literature.

Unit 9 of NE4 gives advice on critical writing about novels.

C. See also CHILDREN'S LITERATURE, CLASS LIBRARY, CLASS READERS, LIBRARY, NOVELS, READING ALOUD, READING LISTS.

Skills

The development and encouragement of certain skills are an important part of the teaching of English. If pupils are to be prepared to play a full and useful part in society when they leave school, they must have a reasonable command of these skills. The basic skills are the ability to read, to write, to talk confidently and fluently, to listen; and much of the work of the English lessons will be directed towards the acquisition of these skills through practice and through the creation of a sympathetic atmosphere within the classroom. The process will be slow and gradual, but the English teacher must never lose sight of this objective.

A. Throughout *New English* there are ample opportunities for developing the skills of reading, writing, talking and listening.

C. See also AIMS OF ENGLISH TEACHING, LISTENING, READING, TALK, WRITING.

Social Studies

To what extent is the study of a theme like crime or marriage or racial prejudice the province of the social studies department and to what extent is it the legitimate concern of the English department? There are many areas where the subject matters of the two departments seem to overlap, and there is certainly a danger with some teachers of English becoming watered down social studies. Many of the topics covered in social studies are matters of general concern about which young people should think and formulate their views and opinions. English is very much the place to discuss and write about these matters as well. The main difference is that social studies is much more occupied with finding out the facts and obtaining a clear picture of the situation whereas English concentrates much more on gaining an insight into questions by looking at literature and at the response of writers, and by encouraging pupils to write creatively and imaginatively about the questions, by putting themselves into the place of people involved, as well as sorting out their own attitudes and opinions.

The social studies department would look at the following aspects of crime, for instance: categories of crime and statistics about crimes committed; current trends in crime; the role of the police and the courts; the causes of crime and its prevention. In English, pupils may read Alan Sillitoe's novel *The Loneliness of the Long-Distance Runner* or Brendan Behan's *Borstal Boy*. They may write about what it is like to commit a crime or be caught or appear in court; or about what it is like to be a policeman or what they think of the police or about some contacts they have had with the police; or they may give their views on capital punishment or the effectiveness of prisons or about what to do about vandalism or football hooligans. Both approaches are valid and indeed could be said to complement each other.

A. Many of the themes looked at in *New English*, particularly in NE4, could equally be dealt with in terms of social studies or of English.

B. For a textbook where it could be argued that the borderline between English and social studies becomes blurred, see *Reflections*, eds. Simon Clements, John Dixon, and Leslie Stratta (OUP)

C. See also AIMS OF ENGLISH TEACHING.

110

Specialist Rooms

With subjects like science and home economics, the need for specialist rooms is obvious. A case can also be made for English to be taught
in specialist rooms. In the first instance, continuity is important. All
the English lessons of a class should be held in the same room so
that books are readily available, so that a class library and reference
books can be properly organized, and so that displays of work and
other material can be put on the walls. Ideally, the English rooms
should be *en suite* so that when appropriate there can be easy inter-
change between teachers and pupils, and so that equipment can be
shared.

Each room should be large (especially if it is envisaged that drama
lessons should take place there) and the furniture should be
manœuvrable and adaptable so that it can be rearranged for group
work or discussion sessions or other activities. There should be
ample cupboard space and display space for the storage of books,
a class library, reference books, pictorial material. A tape recorder,
a cassette recorder, a record player, a camera, a slide projector, a
film projector, a television receiver, a radio, an over-head projector
should all be available. Some method of duplicating material—the
higher the quality the better—should also be available.

B. See:
Head of Department, Michael Marland (Heinemann)

C. See also ACTIVITIES, DISPLAY, DUPLICATED MATERIAL, HEAD OF
DEPARTMENT, RESOURCES.

Speeches

Much talk in the English lessons is inevitably spontaneous, arising
out of reading or out of areas of study initiated by the teacher. But
there should also be a place for the prepared speech. This could be
a talk about a hobby or an interest, a defence of or an attack on
a particular opinion, or a description or an explanation of some area
of knowledge. Speeches or talks like these could be illustrated with
diagrams or pictorial material handed out by the pupil or by specially
made charts or by use of the blackboard. Not all pupils will enjoy
being spotlit by this kind of public appearance, but it is one way
of encouraging confidence and fluency. Each speech could be criti-
cized by the class and marks allotted for such things as fluency,
interest, good use of illustrative material. The reading of speeches

should be discouraged as the purpose of the exercise is to improve the ability to speak clearly and without hesitation about a subject from notes and prior preparation.

Another kind of speech which is useful when there are a few minutes left at the end of a period after the work of the lesson is finished is to ask pupils to speak for a minute without preparation on a subject that is given to them there and then. Suitable subjects would be hair or matchsticks or food. In fact, it doesn't really matter what the subject is so long as the speaker has an inventive enough mind to go on thinking and speaking. Under such circumstances, a minute is a long time, and it is surprising how difficult many pupils find it to keep going. The teacher may have to demonstrate that it can be done. Nevertheless, it is a useful occasional exercise for loosening up minds and tongues in public.

A. The Activities sections of *New English* provide a number of opportunities for pupils to prepare speeches. For instance, in NE1, Unit 5, pupils are invited to bring their pets into school and talk about them.

C. DEBATES, DISCUSSION, LISTENING, ORAL WORK, TALK.

Spelling

There are three approaches to the teaching of spelling. One is to ignore it as something unimportant compared with the need to stimulate vivid creative writing and as something that may even impede the production of such writing. A second approach is to treat each pupil as an individual and to expect him, when work is corrected, to make a list of the words he gets wrong, to learn the correct versions, and to get them right next time. Pupils would keep spelling notebooks; they would refer to them and test each other from the words listed there; they would use dictionaries intensively. The third approach is a systematic and regular study and learning of rules, exceptions, peculiarities, groups of related words, and particularly difficult words.

Most people would agree that the first approach is untenable. Spelling is an important aspect of literacy, and not to prepare pupils to cope with it is to fail in one's duty to them. The second approach, with the pupil finding out for himself and catering for his own needs, is probably the best, but the teacher may not have enough time to devote to this method and the pupil may not be sufficiently motivated to keep up to date with his corrections. The third approach involves much hard effort and the writing of exercises and testing, and there is no guarantee that what has been learned as a drill will have any effect on how pupils spell in their own writing. Nevertheless, it seems that the only possible method of tackling spelling is either the second or the third or a combination of the two.

Nor need learning to spell always be a chore. Tests on spelling and finding more examples of words can appeal to the competitive element in pupils, and some work on spelling can take on the nature of a game. Assignments such as 'Write down as many words as you can using the apostrophe to indicate letters omitted', for instance, or 'Write down as many homophones as you can', or 'Find fifty words containing silent letters' can be stimulating and interesting. Where possible, words should be considered in groups so that they re-enforce each other, for instance, words ending in '—tion' or words beginning with 'exc—' or words with double 'l'. Where possible, words should be used not just learned, and pupils should write sentences containing the words.

Many people claim that the standard of spelling today is much lower than it has been in the past. New methods of teaching pupils how to read have been blamed. Whether this is true or not is difficult to say, but certainly many people seem to have what may be called a deficient visual sense: if asked to read out their own writing, many pupils will read what they meant to write and what they thought they had written, not what they have actually written, and if asked to spell a word they have written, they will read out the correct spelling not the incorrect one on the page. On the other hand, if they are told that they have made a mistake in a particular line of their writing, they can often point it out straightaway. Somehow, teachers have to make pupils more able actually to see the words they read and the words they write; they have to increase the visual awareness of their pupils.

Motivation is a vital element in getting pupils to take more care with spelling. No matter how many drills or spelling lists are worked through, unless pupils see and feel that being able to spell correctly is important, they are unlikely to make much progress. In this respect, social considerations play a large part: being able to write a letter of application for a job; the need to impress when writing a letter to a boy- or girl-friend; the need to avoid embarrassing gaffes in front of colleagues at work. It is then that young people may think more seriously about spelling. In one sense it will be too late because they will have left school, but if guidelines have been laid down and the use of the dictionary encouraged, there may be hope.

113

A. Each unit in *New English* has a section on spelling. An attempt to point out to pupils how important spelling is is given in Unit 1 of NE3.

B. See:
English Language Reference Book, Rhodri Jones (Blackie)
A Spelling Dictionary, Michael West (Longman)
Spelling, G. H. Vallins (Andre Deutsch)
Spelling: Caught or Taught?, M. Peters (Routledge)
Alpha to Omega, Bevé Hornsby and Frula Shear (Heinemann) provides much source material for teaching spelling.

C. See also CORRECTION OF WORK, DICTIONARY.

Spout

This is one method of giving pupils practice in reading aloud. They are asked to choose and prepare a passage or a poem to read to the rest of the class. The pupil should introduce his reading and set it in its context for his audience. Marks can be allocated for appropriateness of choice as well as for ability to put the reading over. Criticisms of the passage and the reading can be invited from the rest of the class. Several periods can be devoted to hearing pupils deliver their spouts or else they can be fitted in a few at a time, perhaps at the end of a lesson. The value of the exercise lies in the fact that pupils have to go to the library to find their own material and they have to be prepared to read aloud as effectively as they can.

The idea is useful in extending and providing further material for a theme. For instance, themes such as the sea, war, love, and marriage would lend themselves particularly well to this approach because of the quantity of material available. If pupils are reading a novel by H. G. Wells or by John Wyndham, they could be asked to find a spout from another novel by the same author. Or pupils could be given a different kind of literary area to explore by being asked to find an extract from science fiction, a description, an account of a character.

Here as an example are some of the poems collected and read by a 4th year class on the theme of town and country. There is some dead wood but the list nevertheless shows an interesting variety.
'On Westminster Bridge' (Wordsworth)
'West Wind' (Masefield)
'The Little Green Orchard' (De la Mare)
'Disobedience' (A. A. Milne)
'Interruption' (Robert Graves)

'The Brook' (Tennyson)
'In Romney Marsh' (John Davidson)
'Early Spring' (W. H. Davies)
'Sunrise on the Hills' (Longfellow)
'Olton Pools' (John Drinkwater)
'On the Downs' (G. K. Chesterton)
'At Chelsea' (Hilary Corke)
'Up on the Downs' (Masefield)
'There is a Hill' (Robert Bridges)
'The Poplar Field' (William Cowper)
'The Lake Isle of Innesfree' (W. B. Yeats)

The heavy reliance on the Georgian poets is perhaps a reflection on the library rather than on the class and points up the need to have a wide range of anthologies and individual poets available for pupils to choose from.

After the readings, poems or extracts could be written out to form an anthology, either in the form of a booklet, or for display on the walls of the classroom.

A. A number of opportunities for pupils to find material of this kind and read it aloud are suggested in the Activities sections of *New English*.

C. See also ANTHOLOGIES, LIBRARY, POETRY, READING ALOUD, THEMES.

Standard English

Much of the work of the English lessons is directed towards ensuring that pupils are able to express themselves in standard English. Yet dialect and natural colloquial speech need not be a barrier to communication and can even have a liveliness and vitality lacking in more formal types of English. So where does the English teacher stand? Examining boards and employers expect pupils and employees to be able to express themselves in what is usually regarded as correct English, and therefore the English teacher has a duty to ensure that their pupils are aware of the requirements and can meet them when necessary. But the power of the vernacular should not be despised or ignored. It is an example of the double view which the English teacher has to be able to sustain—encouraging individual expression while at the same time pointing out its deviation from normally accepted standards.

A. Most of *New English* is inevitably concerned with the rules and regulations of standard English and how to achieve it. For a discussion about dialect and standard English, see NE4, Unit 5.

C. See also DIALECT.

Stimulus

Much of the work of the English lessons, whether it be reading, writing or talking will consist of the pattern of an action followed by a reaction: the teacher provides the stimulus to which the pupil responds. This being so, the teacher must try to vary the stimulus as much as possible so as to ensure that palates do not become jaded. Here are some examples of the kind of stimulus or starting points a teacher could use:

a poem, an extract from a story or a novel or a newspaper to initiate a discussion or a piece of writing;

a discussion or talk about personal experience before writing;

a radio or television programme or a film;

a dramatic improvisation;

music to suggest a mood about which pupils write;

a picture or a photograph as the starting point for writing;

sounds (a knock at the door, the sound of a whistle) to suggest writing;

unusual objects (a piece of machinery, a seashell, a piece of velvet) to call forth a reaction in writing;

school magazines;

literary competitions.

C. See also DISCUSSION, FILMS, MUSIC, PICTURES, SENSES, WRITING.

Stock Room

Every English department needs to have a centrally situated stock room where books and material can be stored and to which teachers have ready access. The stock must be arranged in an easily identifiable way, and there ought to be a system for indicating which material or set of books is out and who has it. This may seem very obvious, but there is nothing more irritating than for a teacher to spend time searching for a particular set of books only to learn that a colleague has it all the time. It is one of the responsibilities of the head of department to ensure that a workable system exists, that books and material are kept in order, and that annual checks are made to see that books have not been lost. Records of stock must also be kept up to date. Alternatively, this is a duty that may be delegated to another member of the department.

Depending on the space available, the stock room could be used as a base for duplicating material and making resources or as an English department office.

B. See:
Head of Department, Michael Marland (Heinemann)

C. See also DUPLICATED MATERIAL, HEAD OF DEPARTMENT, RESOURCES, SPECIALIST ROOMS.

Summary

There is some value in asking pupils to summarize the ideas or arguments expressed in a piece of writing. It is the kind of thing some of them may be called upon to do in later life, and it does test their understanding of the passage. Whether it is necessary to include every idea in the passage or only those relevant to a particular area, and whether it is necessary to be precise about the number of words used are matters that can be discussed. Pupils should be encouraged to read the passage carefully several times, to jot down the main ideas in note form, and then to reconstruct the arguments in clear prose from their notes. In this way, the temptation of simply copying out phrases and sentences from the passage may be avoided.

A. Many of the comprehension questions on passages in *New English* require pupils to summarize information or views.

Surveys

One activity which can be used to gauge classroom opinion and attitudes is the survey. Individual pupils can go round the other members of the class asking questions related to the theme being studied and draw up conclusions from the answers they receive. For instance, if the theme is pets, the survey could take the form of a census of all the pets kept by members of the class and an evaluation of what the most popular pets are. Surveys of this kind can produce interesting information and can lead to fruitful discussion. They also provide a legitimate opportunity for some movement within the

117

classroom and for pupils (especially the less able) to undertake a project which is less dependent on literacy than some others.

A. Many of the Activities sections of *New English* include surveys. For instance, in NE2 Unit 4, there is a survey to find out how many pupils in the class believe in ghosts and why; in NE3, Unit 5, there is a survey to find out how many approve of fox hunting.

C. See also ACTIVITIES.

Syllabus

It is essential that every English department have a published syllabus. Drawing up the syllabus and keeping it up to date ensure that the purpose and aims of English teaching are constantly borne in mind and being revised. The syllabus can inform other teachers in the school of the approach and point of view of the English department. It can also help a new member of the department to understand the attitudes of the department towards the teaching of English and help him to fit in more easily.

There is a difference between a syllabus and a scheme of work. A syllabus outlines the aims of the department and indicates the general framework by which it is hoped that these aims can be achieved. A scheme of work sets out in much greater detail the day-to-day work to be carried out by each class.

Here, as an example, is a syllabus written some years ago. It is not intended as ideal, and if written today, it would probably be considerably different. Indeed, it may be something of a historical document indicating as it does a certain attitude towards the teaching of English at a particular time. However, it could provide a start for an interesting discussion on what an English syllabus should consist of and what the approach to English teaching should be.

English Department Syllabus: Years I to IV

These notes are a summary of our aims and methods as they were evolved during the first year of the comprehensive school (1967–68). They cover points raised, discussed, and generally agreed at departmental meetings throughout the year.

GENERAL APPROACH
1. We approach English not as an academic study but as an arts or *creative subject* based on the exploration of experience through

reading, talking and writing. There are certain areas of utilitarian English 'skills', such as letter-writing, the ability to make clear reports, the documentation of facts, the comprehension and filling in of forms, which have to be considered, but essentially English should encourage the extension of the child's experience and his understanding of himself and the world around him.

2.   Our approach to the teaching of *language* should not be an arid one concerned with grammatical analysis and linguistic questions considered in isolation. It should encourage the pupil to find a language appropriate to the experience he is writing about. The proper use of language helps the child to find significance in his own experiences because it is necessary for him to select, consider, and articulate those experiences in a manner which shows the sincerity and validity of the experiences and which communicates them clearly to the reader. The emphasis is therefore on the pupil's own creative writing and exploration of experience through writing. It follows, then, that work on 'communicative skills' should be based on the pupil's own writing.

3.   *Talking* is as important an element in English work as writing and reading. It is through speech that the first stimulus and response are made, and the pupil is able to share and explore experience through talking as well as writing. Speech should be a collaborative activity, and listening is as important as speaking. For the teacher, it is important to find verbal equivalents for stimuli and creative work, such as the use of personal detail, concrete examples, imagery, etc. For the pupil, we should aim at encouraging in him an ability to express his ideas fluently, coherently and with a proper attempt at articulation equivalent to content, whether it be factual reportage/ opinion or something more dramatic/personal like reading a poem. We should not be aiming at teaching elocution.

4.   The course is *literature-based*. Literature should be used to explore experience in the same way as talking and writing. Through reading, the pupil is able to share in the experience of professional writers and to see that they are doing what he is doing in his own writing: the process of reading and writing becomes two-way. We should be concerned with 'literary criticism' to the extent of considering how the communication of ideas is made more effective or hindered, but we should not be concerned with it in an academic way or as a study in itself. Nor are we concerned with giving an outline of the 'heritage of English literature'. Since the emphasis is on sharing experience, we must choose literature which speaks

119

directly to the pupils and to their own experience. The works chosen should not set up barriers of language or period. It follows, therefore, that emphasis will be on modern writers and works—*The Catcher in the Rye*, not *Silas Marner*; Ted Hughes, not Wordsworth. This does not preclude the use of works by writers such as John Clare, Defoe, Twain, Mayhew, and possibly Shakespeare, which can still speak directly to the pupil's experience; but works requiring a critical or historical perspective for their understanding are not suitable.

5. *Reading* should receive as much emphasis as talking and writing since the ability to understand written matter is a social necessity and since reading is an activity which the pupil is more likely to continue after he leaves school than writing. We must try to encourage our pupils to see reading as a pleasurable as well as useful activity. It must be remembered that a large number of our pupils have difficulty in the sheer mechanical act of reading, and these need particular attention. Some personal motivation or reward must be found to compensate for the difficulty of the task of reading for these children so that they accept the activity as valuable. The development and measurement of *comprehension* should arise from reading (e.g. in the form of reports of research or summarizing for the benefit of others, or in the form of questions based on a central episode in a novel) rather than from isolated comprehension exercises. Much oral work will also inevitably be of a 'comprehension' type.

6. The general approach to the teaching of English in the first four years should be that of the CSE and not the GCE as the former is considered to have a broader basis and is more relevant to life and experience and is therefore of greater educational value.

7. English is of great *social* importance as it is the subject which more than any other prepares the pupil for life.

8. *Language work* must emerge from the children's own writing. Grammar or language exercises in isolation are pointless. The children must first be encouraged to write and to find interest and pleasure in writing, and then deficiencies in communication can be dealt with. The suggested approach is this: lessons should be based on common mistakes collected from written work; dictionaries of common mistakes, commonly misspelt words, points about punctuation, etc. should be made by the children themselves in small vocabulary notebooks.

9. The approach to the *correction of written work* should be one of encouragement. The correction of every grammatical mistake,

particularly with weak pupils, is likely to have a depressing and discouraging effect. Four or five mistakes marked on each piece of writing is quite sufficient. These can then be discussed with the child individually, or, if they are common mistakes, with the class as a whole. Insistence on correctness of expression is likely to have an inhibiting effect. Be thankful for what you get and praise as much as you can. Every child must be given the chance of success in whatever sphere he is able to achieve it.

10. All creative written work should be done in *loose-leaf folders.* Children should be encouraged to regard these as important collections of their work, to decorate and illustrate their writing, and generally produce an attractive book which can give pleasure to others and of which they can be proud. Children should be encouraged to find material and illustrations relevant to their writing from newspapers and magazines to add to their folders.

11. *Walls* in classrooms should be used as means of displaying work done, together with illustrative material, so that other children can enjoy and appreciate the work done. This can act as an incentive to the children whose work is displayed as well as providing a purpose and an audience for the work instead of it being done in a vacuum.

12. The *school magazine* 'Reflection' should be regarded as another means of providing children with an audience and a chance of success. The standard of the school magazine reflects the teaching of the English Department.

13. Another method of approach which should be used is the making of books on a single topic to which all children in the group contribute, e.g. a series of articles and illustrations on 'Holidays', a collection of poems about the sea. These can then be placed in the library for the benefit and interest of other children.

14. *Stimuli* other than literature should be used as much as possible to spark off discussion and writing, e.g. music, pictures, films, recordings, live animals and exhibits, outside visits (e.g. to the zoo, to the fire station), drama, etc.

15. The role of the *library* is vital in the teaching of English. Children should be encouraged to accept the idea that books are useful and can give pleasure. Work involving children doing their own research on particular topics should be encouraged—though this is hindered at the moment by inadequate library facilities.

16.   *Departmental meetings* are held once a month, usually the last Thursday in the month to discuss policy and problems.

The Thematic Approach

Teaching throughout the first four years is based on the thematic approach.

METHOD

1   A theme (e.g. 'Getting into Trouble', 'The Supernatural', 'The Sea') should be chosen which has scope for development, is suitable for and is likely to be of interest and value to the particular group, and for which there is material available.

2.   A poem or a story can act as an effective start to the theme, but however started, as much literature as possible which sheds light on the topic should be introduced to stimulate discussion and writing. Where necessary, material should be duplicated and then stored in the stock cupboard so that it is available to all. Because of the shortage of money to buy sufficient readers, anthologies, etc., and because of the inadequacy of most current text-books, much duplicating of material, though demanding in the finding and the duplicating, will be necessary and is very important.

3.   Out of the theme should emerge a series of assignments involving discussion and writing. These should take the form of:
a)   argumentative (e.g. Should the police be armed?)
b)   factual (e.g. What is the purpose of the prison service?)
c)   imaginative (e.g. Imagine you are in the condemned cell. Describe your last night before execution.)
d)   the writing of poetry, particularly free verse (e.g. Write a poem about an occasion when you felt guilty.)
e)   the conducting of polls (e.g. What are the chief causes of friction between children and parents in your form?)
f)   research into some area of the topic (e.g. Find out what you can about the RSPCA.)
g)   comprehension (e.g. What do we learn from Vernon Scannell's poem 'A Case of Murder' of the reasons for cruelty?)
Research on the topic should involve use of the library and the collection of material from newspapers and magazines, the finding of poems on the topic to copy into folders and to read to the class, the writing of letters and sending away for information, etc.

4.   The amount of time spent by a group on a particular theme will depend on the value of the topic itself, the amount of material available and the interest of the group. It might be two weeks; it might be two months.

5.   A theme may give rise to 20 assignments. The method of dealing with these is at the discretion of the teacher. He may give the children a free choice as to how many they do and in which order; or he may insist that certain assignments are compulsory and others a free choice.

6.   The work done in Drama should be a continuation of the exploratory theme in terms of movement, improvisation, etc. Close cooperation is therefore necessary between the teacher of English and the teacher of Drama of a particular group where these are not the same person.

7.   The organization of work on the theme principle does not preclude occasional work on subjects outside the theme, e.g. a snowfall or a fire may be of such immediate interest as to cause the topic to be interrupted for the benefit of this more immediate stimulus; an event in national or school life may call for attention; a book unrelated to any topic may be read for pleasure; the group may embark on an extended piece of writing such as a novel, an autobiography, etc.

ADVANTAGES

1.   The thematic approach provides a framework which unifies the work of the English Department but which allows the individual teacher to develop his work to suit his own ideas and tastes within that framework.

2.   It supplies a unity to the work done with a particular group in the English lessons.

3.   It allows subjects to be developed and explored in greater depth than is otherwise usual in English teaching.

4.   All the skills and qualities which the teaching of English hopes to encourage are developed and extended within the thematic framework—reading, talking, creative writing, factual reports, letter writing, research, comprehension.

5.   It is a system which is particularly adaptable to mixed ability groups.

6.   The method is also one which lends itself to team teaching and

to the extension of work to include a number of different subject departments, e.g. a film could be shown to a whole year which could then split into different groups to explore different aspects of the theme under study, coming together at various times to report back to the whole year; or historical, geographical, artistic, or moral aspects of the theme could be explored in other subject periods. Experiments of this kind are to be encouraged.

Mixed Ability Groups

1. This is what comprehensive education is about—at least as far as English is concerned. Children of all types should be able to learn about and from each other. It is hoped that the weaker children will benefit from the greater accuracy and reasoning power of the more academic children and that the more academic children will gain something from the generally less inhibited and more imaginative less academic children.

2. A group consisting solely of lower ability children is likely to behave like a group of lower ability children. There is no example or incentive for improvement and little chance for individual attention. In a mixed ability group, it should be easier for weak children to receive individual attention while the other children continue with some other work, and it is hoped that the example of other children working will encourage them.

3. When it comes to imaginative work, there is little difference between top and bottom stream children; both are capable of producing interesting and exciting work—the only difference is the degree of correctness (but even this is usually no barrier to communication). Correlation with subjects like art, music, and drama is relevant here since we regard English as a creative subject and not an academic one.

4. Where a number of subjects are taught in mixed ability groups, this should provide the children, particularly the less stable ones, with a greater sense of security and a stronger sense of belonging, which are essential before the children can be expected to settle down happily to work.

5. The topic method is easily adaptable to mixed ability groups. Most children, of whatever level, are able to contribute something to oral discussion; all children are able to produce something in the way of imaginative writing in response to a stimulus; much of the

modern literature used appeals to all children. The method allows children to work at different rates, and the bright child would not be penalised as he would be expected to cover more ground, do more work, and explore the topic in greater depth than other children.

ADAPTING THE THEMATIC APPROACH TO MIXED ABILITY GROUPS
1. Stimuli can be presented to and imaginative writing can be tackled by the group as a whole. Much reading, if carefully chosen, can be done by the group as a whole. The same is true of much discussion work.

2. Much group work within the group must be encouraged, e.g. discussions among small groups with one acting as secretary for the group and reporting back findings to the complete group; bright pupils should be encouraged to read more widely and to read more difficult books and report back to the whole group, perhaps making a summary of the book and reading selected extracts; research projects can be undertaken in small groups, the tasks graded according to the ability of the groups; children can correct each other's work, though tact may be needed here; the weaker children can have individual attention on the language side of their work while the others do other work.

THEMES
Themes in Years One and Two should be designed to extend the child's experience of himself and of his more immediate environment. The kind of areas which should be covered are:
The Elements—Fire, Water, the Sea, etc.
Weathers—Snow, Fog, Wind, Rain, Winter Weather, etc.
The Seasons
Surroundings—The Family, Pets, My Street, My Town, etc.
Town and Country
The Imagination—Fantasy, The Supernatural, The Uncanny, The Unknown, Foreign Places and Times, The Senses, Night and Dreams, etc.
Animals—Predators, Wild and Tame, Cruelty to Animals, Hunting, etc.
Human Achievement—Adventure, Danger, Escape, Pioneering, Transport, etc.

Themes in Years Three and Four should take into consideration the growing maturity of the pupil and the increasing complexity of his emotional response, relating this on broader lines to man's place in society, and to a consideration of the outside commercial, political and social pressures which are exerted on him. The kinds of areas which should be covered are:

Man and Society—Outcasts and Rejects, Racial Discrimination, Authority and the Individual, Class, etc.

People at Work and Play—Attitudes to Work, Leisure, etc.

War—Cowardice and Bravery, Civilians, etc.

Feelings—Loneliness, Guilt, Fear, etc.

Growing Up—Childhood, Adolescence, Parents, Old People, etc.

Love and Marriage

Personal Relationships—Conflict, Friendship, etc.

The Law—Crime and Punishment, Being in Trouble, The Police, etc.

Change

The Modern World—Advertising, Newspapers, Current Events, Violence, Famine, etc.

CSE type work on particular books.

Also included in the syllabus, but not reproduced here, were a list of recommended reading for teachers, a list of reading material and resources available for pupils, and a series of worksheets outlining various themes (including suitable reading and discussion and writing assignments) devised by various members of the department and available for all to use.

C. See also AIMS OF ENGLISH TEACHING, DEPARTMENTAL MEETING, HEAD OF DEPARTMENT.

Talk

The English lessons ought to provide the ideal opportunity for pupils to talk. The atmosphere should be such that they feel free to express their opinions and formulate their ideas. The teacher must be receptive and sympathetic: any suggestion of patronage about or contempt for what is being expressed would be disastrous. What pupils have to say is just as important as what the teacher has to communicate: in the English classroom, all should have an equal right to express themselves.

Talk can take many forms, and pupils should have the chance to take part in and experiment with as large a variety as possible. There is the casual conversation about the day's events; there is the discussion about poems, plays and novels being read; there is the exchange of opinion about current affairs; there is the formulation of views or the passing on of information about a theme under consideration; there are debates and speeches, the giving of instructions and reports, the give and take of question and answer.

In talk, the teacher tends to be the initiator and centre, and perhaps this is necessary if a disciplined and constructive atmosphere is to be maintained. But talk has really taken off if pupils are able to exchange views with each other without having to go through the intermediary of the teacher. Again, the teacher may sometimes feel it necessary to rephrase what a pupil has said, either to make sure that other pupils have heard it or to make sure that the meaning is clearly expressed. This is a temptation that should be resisted. Allow the pupils as far as possible to say what they think or feel in their own honest, if sometimes unvarnished, way. Where there is a danger of inaudibility, ensure that the discipline or atmosphere in the class is such that proper respect is being paid to what is being said and arrange the furniture in such a way that oral contact is easy between pupils. The teacher, of course, has an important role in drawing out pupils—in asking them to expand on what they have said or to give examples; to turn the talk to other pupils by asking if they agree or disagree with what has been said; to add his own views or experiences or information.

Talk need not always be a full classroom activity. It can also be organized in groups. It depends on the kind of talk taking place, but there is sometimes a danger of one or two individuals monopolizing the situation. When the discussion is broken down into groups, there is more possibility of other individuals taking part.

It should be remembered that for many pupils, the occasions for talk with their teachers, and particularly their English teachers, may well be the only contacts that they have where they can express their views and have them listened to, and where they can hear an adult's considered response. This kind of exchange is invaluable in the process of growing up, and it is the English teacher's responsibility to see that it takes place.

A. There are many opportunities for talk of different kinds to emerge out of the suggestions and assignments in *New English*.

B. See:
Talking and Writing, ed. James Britten (Methuen)
Talk: A Practical Guide to Oral Work in the Secondary School, David Self (Ward Lock)
Speak for Yourselves, J. W. Casciani (Harrap)

C. See also DEBATES, DISCUSSION, GROUP WORK, LISTENING, ORAL WORK, PRONUNCIATION, SPEECHES, TAPE RECORDING.

Tape Recording

The tape recorder or cassette recorder can be an invaluable aid in English teaching. Radio programmes, plays, and records can be recorded for use in the classroom. Classroom discussions and talks can be recorded for playing back and criticizing. Interviews can be recorded to play in class or to provide information. Plays, talks, advertisements can be made for the radio medium and recorded on tape. It can thus provide opportunities for writers, speakers, and technicians. In some schools it is even possible to go further and to produce daily radio programmes in the form of magazines or music request programmes. The extent to which tape recording can be used will, of course, depend on the resources of the school and the interests of individual teachers, but the recorder is an essential part of the equipment of the English department, and its use can stimulate much interesting work, especially with pupils who are more ready or able to talk than write.

A. The Activities sections of *New English* suggest opportunities for the use of the tape or cassette recorder. For example, in Unit 2 of NE1, it is suggested that pupils could ask their parents or grandparents for their impressions of what schools were like in their day and the results could be recorded on a cassette recorder; in Unit 1 of NE2, pupils are asked to record the impressions of their parents of how the area they live in has changed over the past twenty or thirty years.

B. See:
Teaching with Tape, J. Graham Jones (Focal Press)

C. See also RADIO.

Teachers' Centre

A well-organized and well-equipped teachers' centre can be a real blessing to the teacher of English—and of other subjects. It should provide him with a reference library where he is able to check up on the latest research on the teaching of English and where he can examine educational editions of novels, poetry anthologies and textbooks currently available. There should be facilities for photocopying and duplicating material to provide attractive worksheets for his classes. There should be courses organized by the centre or by teachers or by the English advisor; there should be visiting speakers and discussion groups on matters of current importance such as mixed ability teaching, the role of literature, multi-racial education, and so on. The centre should provide the English teacher with the opportunity to play an active part in influencing attitudes towards the teaching of English in the area and enable him to learn about the practice in other schools. Often, teachers work in isolation, ploughing their lonely furrow, cut off from their colleagues: the teachers' centre can be a meeting place where they can come into contact with other teachers and discuss, argue, and learn about what goes on in other schools so that their own teaching can be enriched and improved.

Team Teaching

The use of team teaching in English can provide for an exciting and stimulating experience both for pupils and for teachers. Pupils can benefit from a greater variety of work and groupings; teachers can be more actively involved in selecting and organizing teaching material and in discussing the work and progress with colleagues. Team teaching can also be an economic way of providing resource material with individual teachers being responsible for a particular area of research and then producing material which the other members of the team can use.

Team teaching may take the form of a project or a theme with a lead-lesson when the whole group is together (this may be an illustrated talk or lecture, a film or a visit) after which smaller groups follow up different aspects of the subject. Follow-up work can involve research, creative writing, reading, the provision of display material, the finding of further resources, tape recording, drama, visits. Groups can move from teacher to teacher either in a firmly controlled sequence or on a freer and more voluntary basis. It is useful to have a remedial teacher as one of the team to give a helping hand to pupils who may be having difficulties. In fact, the team teaching approach may be one of the ways in which mixed ability teaching can succeed and in which the brighter pupils have a chance to be fully stretched.

At the end of the project, some way should be found of gathering the different strands together, perhaps by another plenary session where each group reports back on what it has been doing or by an exhibition or a magazine or a written report.

Team teaching can be undertaken on an inter-disciplinary basis where a subject lends itself to different approaches—historical, geographical, religious, social, scientific as well as in terms of English skills and concerns.

Good organization is vital for the success of team teaching. The project must be discussed by the teachers concerned, areas of responsibility and aims must be clearly understood, resource material must be available when required. Where possible, a period on the timetable should be set aside when all the teachers involved are available so that discussion, preparation, modification and forward planning can take place. Suitable accommodation (perhaps the library and a number of adjoining classrooms) and generous staffing (so that groups can be as small as possible) are also highly desirable. Some form of assessment or record-keeping is needed to ensure that a clear picture is gained of the work a pupil does and the progress he makes as he moves from one aspect of the project or one group to another: there is always a danger with this kind of work that individual pupils can get lost.

A. It would be possible to take one of the themes presented in *New English* and by reorganizing and expanding the material treat it as the basis for team teaching.

B. See:
Team Teaching in Britain, John Freeman (Ward Lock)
Team Teaching and the Teaching of English, Anthony Adams (Wheaton)

C. See also GROUP WORK, MIXED ABILITY, THEMES.

Television

Since watching television occupies so much of the lives of many of our pupils, it is surprising that the medium is not brought more into English lessons. It is clearly an admirable subject for discussion. Advertising, standards, comparison of different programmes and different channels, the amount of time devoted to different kinds of programmes, censorship, violence and sex, the effect on crime, the view of the police presented, news, children's programmes: these are some of the areas that can be explored. Ask pupils to watch a particular programme which can be discussed in class. Find out about favourite television programmes. Discuss the ratings and why certain programmes are popular.

It is possible also to read some published television scripts and to discuss television technique. Most television studios welcome school visits. The knowledge of the various stages of a production gained from a visit of this kind can be invaluable. Pupils can be encouraged to write their own plays or scenes for television or advertisements. If the school is lucky enough to have its own television equipment, practical work in making a television programme can be undertaken. Since television is such an important medium, pupils ought to be in a position to look at it critically.

B. The following books contain scripts of television plays and programmes:

Softly, Softly, Elwyn Jones (Longman)
The Pressures of Life, ed. Michael Marland (Longman)
Scene Scripts, ed. Michael Marland (Longman)
Z cars, ed. Michael Marland (Longman)
Conflicting Generations, ed. Michael Marland (Longman)
Steptoe and Son, Ray Galton and Alan Simpson (Longman)
See also *The TV/Film Script*, Rodney Bennett (Harrap)
Teaching Television, (ILEA Publishing Centre, Highbury Station Road, London N1 1SB)

C. See also ADVERTISEMENTS, RADIO.

Ten Essential Poems

If a pupil were to be restricted to only ten poems during his school career (which heaven forbid!), which ten poems would you choose? My choice would be as follows:
'Snake', D. H. Lawrence
'The Unknown Citizen', W. H. Auden
'O What is that Sound?' W. H. Auden
'Child on Top of a Greenhouse', Theodore Roethke
'The Horses', Edwin Muir
'Your Attention Please', Peter Porter
'Preludes', T. S. Eliot
'Dulce et Decorum Est', Wilfred Owen
'Hawk Roosting', Ted Hughes
'Cynddylan on a Tractor', R. S. Thomas.

'Snake' tells how Lawrence threw a piece of wood at a snake and then regretted his mean action. It shows the conflict in twentieth-century man between his instinct to worship what is beautiful and the voice of education which inhibits him with warnings and repressions.

'The Unknown Citizen' describes the average man who is so conformist that he has become faceless, a mere number.

'O What is that Sound?' tells of the approach of enemy soldiers and the betrayal of trust when the loved one deserts.

'Child on Top of a Greenhouse' describes the sense of guilt that a boy feels when he has done something wrong—even the chrysanthemums 'stare up like accusers'.

'The Horses' deals with a situation in the future when most of the world has been destroyed and the survivors try to return to a primitive innocence and simplicity.

'Your Attention Please' is a satirical account of a broadcaster giving instructions during a four-minute warning and indicates the futility of such instructions.

'Preludes' presents a bleak picture of squalid city life.

'Dulce et Decorum Est' describes an episode in the First World War when a soldier is gassed and demonstrates the hollowness of the idea that dying for your country is glorious.

'Hawk Roosting' portrays the arrogance and obsession with power of the hawk, a situation which can be applied to man.

'Cynddylan on a Tractor' is an ironic picture of new-mechanized man.

These descriptions, of course, grossly oversimplify the poems, but each of them presents ideas which remain relevant to young people growing up today and refute the concept that poetry is remote from life and reality. It could be an interesting exercise to draw up your own list of ten essential poems and see whether your pupils have a chance of coming in contact with them and studying them.

C. See also ANTHOLOGIES, POETRY.

Theatre

See DRAMA, PLAYS, SCHOOL PLAYS, SHAKESPEARE, VISITS.

Themes

Using a particular theme or topic can allow the teacher and the class to explore an area of experience in depth. All the English work of a class can be related to this theme or topic—all the reading, writing, talking, drama, and comprehension. This gives a unity to the work of the English lessons which might otherwise be missing. Instead of reading an adventure story and the next few poems in the class anthology, whatever they might be, writing about first experiences at school or a story beginning 'I could feel the cold air on my face ...' discussing the pros and cons of experimenting on animals and doing improvisations on the family at breakfast, *all* the work of the English lesson could be related. *All* the activities could be directed towards examining our experience of the sea or the family or the world of work, taking into account what authors and poets have said about it and what knowledge we can share with other members of the class, so that a much deeper awareness of the subject can emerge and so that what pupils read and write and talk about can have a greater cohesion and relevance.

There are a number of different methods of initiating a theme. You may start by reading a poem, or use the class reader as the starting point. You may choose to lead off with a news item or a point for discussion. You need not even inform the class that they have embarked on the study of a particular theme: it may be something that emerges in the course of the work.

As much literature as possible, relevant to the theme, should be injected into it, either from books or as duplicated material. This could take the form of poems, newspaper articles, statistics, visual material, class readers, and private reading. Written work should try to include different kinds of writing: argumentative, factual, imaginative, the writing of poetry, research, the conducting of surveys, comprehension. The written work could be doled out a piece at a time, or it could be in the form of twelve or so assignments from which pupils choose six to complete in their own time and at their own rate.

The amount of time spent on a theme will depend on the nature of the theme, the quantity of material available, and the interest of the class. It might be two weeks; it might be two months.

Using the thematic approach to organize the work of the class does not preclude occasional work on subjects outside the particular theme being examined. For instance, a snow fall or a fire might be of such immediate interest as to cause the theme to be interrupted in favour of this more vital stimulus. An event in school or national life might call for attention. A book unrelated to the topic might be embarked upon simply for pleasure. The need for a special lesson on common spelling mistakes or a revision of how to write sentences may become apparent.

Here is an example of one theme used with a 4th-year class. The subject was work. *Billy Liar* by Keith Waterhouse was used as the class reader, and we looked particularly at the frustrations which affected Billy at his job with the undertakers. Other literature read and discussed included the interview with the Careers Officer in *A Kestrel for a Knave* by Barry Hines, the short story *The Bike* by Alan Sillitoe, some of Mayhew's interviews with Victorian workers in *London Labour and London Poor*, extracts from George Orwell's *Down and Out in Paris and London* and from Alan Sillitoe's *Saturday Night and Sunday Morning*, and the following poems: 'Toads' (Philip Larkin), 'The Sluggard' (Isaac Newton), 'Work' (D. H. Lawrence), 'The Song of the Wagon Driver' (B. S. Johnson), 'Roman Wall Blues' (W. H. Auden), 'One Tired Housewife' (Anon.), 'The House-wife' (Michael Baldwin), 'Low Seam Worker' (Robert Morgan), 'The Collier's Wife' (D. H. Lawrence), 'Jones the Grocer' (Robert Williams), 'Out, out —' (Robert Frost), 'Last Lesson of the After-noon' (D. H. Lawrence), 'The Man in the Bowler Hat' (A. S. J. Tessimond) and 'The Unknown Citizen' (W. H. Auden).

The starting point was a discussion on how much people earned, whether they deserved the money they got, and how much they ought to be paid. Figures considered were bank managers, pop stars, hair-dressers, nurses, footballers, dustmen, soldiers, policemen, teachers, building labourers, and members of Parliament. Another area discussed was the factors people considered when they chose jobs (assuming that they had a choice)—things like security, hours of work, holidays, opportunities to travel, chances for promotion, responsibility, working conditions and surroundings, the physical effort involved, enjoyment, whether a job is socially helpful and desirable, etc. Other points for discussion which came up in the course of the theme were: the position of the housewife (should she receive a wage?); the topic of equal pay and equal opportunity; the role of the unions and the justification (or otherwise) for strikes; the question of unemployment and of automation.

The literature read presented views on a number of different aspects of work such as job satisfaction, careers advice, the mono-tony of many jobs, the dangers of some jobs, etc.

Out of this talking and reading and more talking emerged a series of written assignments from which pupils were expected to complete seven. They were as follows:
1. Monday Morning.
2. The Dead-End Job.
3. Imagine that you get the sack or are made redundant. Describe your feelings and how you break the news to your family.
4. Write a poem about the feelings of someone who is working

away from home (e.g. a soldier, a commercial traveller, a labourer, a nurse).

5.   Write a reply to the poem 'The Sluggard'.

6.   The Accident. Write a story about an accident that occurs at work (e.g. a mining disaster, or someone getting his arm caught in a machine) and your reactions to it.

7.   A Dangerous Job. A poem or a story.

8.   Strike. Describe a strike meeting—try to catch the emotion of the crowd. Or a story about the family reactions when the bread-winner is on strike.

9.   Late for Work.

10.   First Job.

11.   Write about your experiences in your spare-time job, e.g. as a paper boy, a shop assistant, a messenger.

12.   Give your impressions of the people who come down your street and their jobs, e.g. the postman, the milkman, the paraffin man, the dustman, the policeman, the rag and bone man, the ice cream man. Or write a description of one of them, perhaps as a poem.

13.   Write a description of a shop and shopkeeper that you know well.

14.   Write an interview with a modern workman—a modern Mayhew.

15.   Find a picture of someone at work and write about it—perhaps a poem, a story, or a description.

It could be argued that this particular theme of work encroaches on the province of the careers teacher or on that of the social studies department, but the theme is being approached in a different way. It is being approached through the medium of literature, through the words and imaginations of writers who have something important to say about the subject. Imaginative writing and discussion enable pupils to put themselves in the place of other people and to try to recreate the kind of lives they lead. This is part of what English teaching should be about.

A particular value of the thematic approach is that it can work well with mixed ability classes. Stimuli can be presented to and imaginative writing can be tackled by the group as a whole. Much reading, if carefully chosen, can be done as a shared experience. The same is true of discussion work and drama where the less able can often make a very valuable contribution. If writing is given in the form of assignments, pupils can work at their own individual rates and can be expected to work up to the ability presumed of them. Brighter pupils can be expected to read more widely and to read more difficult books and perhaps report back to the class as a whole. Research projects can be undertaken in groups, the tasks graded according to the ability of the groups. Weaker pupils can receive individual attention while the class as a whole is engaged in writing assignments.

The choice of a particular theme depends on the class and the material available. Here is a list of themes that could be considered appropriate for particular age-groups.

In the 1st and 2nd years, themes should be designed to extend the child's experience of himself and his immediate environment. They include such things as:

the elements—fire, water, the sea, etc.;

weather—snow, fog, wind, rain, etc.;

the seasons;

surroundings—the family, pets, my street, my town, the country;

the imagination—fantasy, the supernatural, the unknown, foreign places and times, the senses, night and dreams;

animals—predators, wild and tame, cruelty to animals, hunting;

human achievement—adventure, danger, escape, pioneering, transport, etc.

Some of these themes could still be suitable for classes in the 3rd year, but by this stage and in years 4 and 5 care has to be taken of the growing maturity of pupils and the increasing complexity of their emotional response. Greater attention should be paid to relating this response to the broader lines of man's place in society and to a consideration of the outside commercial, political, and social pressures that are exerted on man. The kinds of areas that could be covered are:

man and society—outcasts and rejects, racial discrimination, authority and the individual, class;

people at work and play—attitudes to work, leisure;

war—cowardice and bravery, civilians, etc.;

feelings—loneliness, guilt, fear, etc.;

growing up—childhood, adolescence, parents, old people;

personal relationships—love and marriage, friendship, conflict;

the law—crime and punishment, getting into trouble, the police;

the modern world—advertising, newspapers, television, current events, violence, poverty, conservation.

The danger with the thematic approach is that any literature may be reduced simply to being a source of information about the particular theme. But there is no reason why any novel or poem used because it sheds some light on the topic being considered should not also be explored more fully as a novel or a poem and for the other ideas and insights that it contains.

A.   Each unit in *New English* is based on a theme with the reading, writing, discussion, and activities related to and illustrating that theme. Where possible, the language, vocabulary, and spelling work also arises out of the theme or out of literature related to the theme.

There is plenty of scope for the teacher to contribute his own material to the theme and to expand it. In particular, a class reader could be chosen from the Reading Lists supplied which could complement the theme; poems, relevant newspaper articles, extracts from other books could be read and discussed. The suggestions for discussion and writing could also be modified or added to.

B.   For further discussion of the thematic approach and other examples, see:
Topics in English, Geoffrey Summerfield (Batsford)
Teaching by Topics, Peter Rance (Ward Lock)
Children and Themes, Alan Lynskey (OUP)
Creative Themes, Henry Pluckrose (Evans)
For collections of material that would be particularly helpful in developing themes, see:
Themes, ed. Rhodri Jones (Heinemann)
Preludes, ed. Rhodri Jones (Heinemann)
Impact Books, R. H. Poole and P. J. Shepherd (Heinemann)
Dimensions, ed. John L. Foster and Mike Samuda (Wheaton)
The Explorations Series (Wheaton)
The English Project (Ward Lock)

C.   See also MIXED ABILITY, SYLLABUS, TEAM TEACHING

Visits

Any excuse for getting pupils out of the classroom is to be seized—provided there are good educational reasons for it. The purpose may be to study traffic or a shopping centre, to visit a fire-station or a building site, to go to the zoo or an art gallery, so that research can be done and material gathered for discussion and writing. Cinemas and theatres showing films and plays relevant to the work of the class form another category of places to visit. Teachers can sometimes forget that many children are not taken to the theatre by their parents, and a school visit may be the only chance they have of experiencing this social and aesthetic event. Many may never go to the theatre again, but one or two may find the experience one which they wish to renew on their own.

Whatever the visit, preparation is essential. Reasonable behaviour has to be insisted on—this is social training as well as part of English studies—and pupils must be primed about what to expect and what to look for. For some visits, prepared worksheets with questions which pupils have to fill in may provide a focus and a sense of purpose. Some kind of follow-up in the form of discussion or writing or further reading or embarking on a theme is essential if the visit is not to appear a rather pointless exercise and an excuse for getting out of lessons.

A. Some visits are suggested in the Activities sections of *New English*, for example, a visit to a local street-market in Unit 8 of NE1, and a visit to a fishing port or a life-boat station in Unit 2 of NE2.

C. See also RESEARCH.

Vocabulary

Much of the work of English is concerned with looking at words and learning about words and how they are used. It is rather naïve to assume that pupils will extend their own vocabularies simply by reading. The teacher has to play a more active part in drawing the pupils' attention to words and the way they work and in introducing pupils to new words. This can involve looking at the meaning of roots from Latin and Greek; building up words by using different prefixes and suffixes and seeing how these affect the meaning; finding words which have come into English from French, German, Italian, etc.; collecting neologisms and invented words and words derived from places and people's names; explaining the difference in meaning of various close synonyms and antonyms; making lists of various foods or diseases or geographical terms or sporting terms; finding and explaining examples of slang and colloquial speech; looking up the meanings of foreign phrases, abbreviations, and acronyms; explaining idiomatic expressions and proverbial sayings; noting words that have an onomatopoeic effect or whose origin is due to this; checking on words from the pupils' own reading, consulting dictionaries and writing the words and their meanings into vocabulary notebooks. These suggestions indicate some of the lines of inquiry about words which can be initiated. They also show how lively a study of words can be and how this study can help a pupil to extend his own vocabulary.

There should be much recourse to reference books such as the dictionary, *Roget's Thesaurus*, *Brewer's Dictionary of Phrase and*

Fable, Payton's Proper Names, etc. Not only does this extend the pupils' vocabulary, but it also accustoms them to the idea that books are there to be used.

It is important that words discussed in vocabulary lessons should become the personal property of pupils and should be incorporated into their writing. Words should not be discussed in isolation. Asking pupils to write sentences containing the words is an obvious way of re-enforcing the knowledge gained. Occasionally pupils could be asked to write something in the course of which they use ten given words. There is no guarantee that words discussed in vocabulary lessons will enter into the natural vocabulary which pupils use, but there is more likelihood of this happening if words and their meanings are a normal and regular part of the work of the English lessons. Ideas can only be expressed if there are words at hand in which to express them, and it is the duty of the English teacher to ensure that pupils are properly equipped.

A. Each unit of *New English* contains a Vocabulary section in which pupils' attention is directed towards words in the ways indicated.

B. See:
Language Across the Curriculum, Michael Marland (Heinemann)

C. See also DICTIONARY, REFERENCE BOOKS.

Writing

One of the aims of English teaching is to ensure that pupils are able to write coherently, fluently, and accurately so that they can communicate with others in this medium. In later life, the writing a pupil may be asked to perform may be restricted to filling in forms or writing reports or corresponding with relations, but that is no reason for restricting the kind of writing he does in school to these categories. Writing ought to provide an opportunity for expanding a pupil's awareness in all kinds of directions—personal, intellectual, social, aesthetic. The variety of different genres of writing a pupil should experiment with and experience is very wide. It includes autobiography, fiction, poetry, report-making, summarizing, expressing opinions and presenting arguments, letter-writing, description, dialogue, plays, character sketches, interviews, critical writing.

Not all pupils are going to be keen to write, possibly because when they do, their inadequacies in terms of spelling and sentence structure are revealed. There has to be a balance on the teacher's part between encouragement and fault-finding. Clearly, a story which is returned covered in red corrections is unlikely to stimulate a pupil to write another story with any kind of enjoyment; on the other hand, the teacher can't blithely ignore technical deficiencies and misguide the pupil about the quality of his work. First must come a desire to communicate on the pupil's side, and then a desire to improve the skill with which he communicates. The first aim, therefore, is to help the pupil produce in quantity, and then at a later stage to look at the quality. Correction in the first instance is likely to be concerned with content rather than with expression.

One way of encouraging pupils to write is by making them appreciate the pleasures and purpose of writing. If the teacher ensures that he is a constantly receptive audience, then half the battle is won. But the teacher should not be the sole audience. There should be opportunities for the pupil to write for other pupils, to outside agencies, for parents, etc. Rewarding good writing by reading it out, or pinning it on the classroom wall, or duplicating it, or printing it in a magazine can provide further stimulus.

Another important factor is to make sure that there is a variety of writing assignments. They should not always be stories or factual accounts. The starting off point should also be varied. Writing can emerge out of reading, discussion, unusual objects in the classroom, music, visits. The quality of the stimulus, whatever it may be, can be instrumental in the quality of the writing produced and in providing a fresh impetus for jaded writers.

A. There are many opportunities for writing in *New English*. As well as the Writing Assignments given in each unit, there are questions on the extracts used and suggestions for expressing personal opinions. The Activities sections also indicate some assignments which could be written or oral.

B. For further views on writing, see:
Talking and Writing, ed. James Britten (Methuen)
Directions in the Teaching of English, ed. Denys Thompson (CUP)
English Teaching, Arthur Rowe (Hart Davis)
Every English Teacher, Anthony Adams and John Pearce (OUP)
Teaching English, J. H. Walsh (Heinemann)
Understanding Children Writing (Penguin)
For examples of children's writing, see
Children as Writers (Heinemann)
Enjoying Writing, ed. A. B. Clegg (Hart Davis)
The World in a Classroom, ed. Chris Searle (Writers and Readers Publishing Cooperative)

C. See also AUDIENCES, COMPENDIUMS, COMPREHENSION, CORREC-
TION OF WORK, FREE WRITING, PERSONAL WRITING, REPAIR WORK,
SHORT STORIES, STIMULUS, SUMMARY, WRITING POETRY.

Writing Poetry

Pupils may object to being asked to write poetry on the grounds
that they are not going to be poets when they grow up. But that
is not the point. Writing poetry is a valuable activity in extending
a pupil's ability to use language and to give shape to experience as
well as giving him an insight into how a poet works. If a pupil is
encouraged to write poetry as a natural part of the work of the
English lessons in the early years, then there is unlikely to be much
resistance later on. Difficulty usually arises only where pupils in the
4th or 5th years are suddenly asked to write poetry having had no
previous experience of how to set about it.

The simplest process is to begin with examples of poems which
pupils can study and then adapt to their own needs. This does not
necessarily lead to imitative work. The poems are there to provide
a pattern so that pupils have an idea of the form into which they
can put their own ideas.

Although most pupils tend to think that all poems rhyme, it is
usually best to start with free verse. This provides more freedom and
avoids the danger of silly rhymes determining how the poem goes.
The poems of D. H. Lawrence provide good examples here (poems
like 'Bat' or 'Mountain Lion' or 'Snake'). Read the poem to the class.
Point out the different lengths of the lines and the different effects
these have. Then suggest that pupils write a similar poem on any
subject of their own choice, not bothering with rhyme and taking a
new line and starting a new verse whenever they feel the sense
requires it. The teacher may have to suggest some subjects such as the
seasons, different kinds of weather or physical activities, a crowded
scene or a workshop or an engine. There may be some protests at
first, but it is usually surprising how readily pupils apply themselves
to the task and how effective the results of their efforts can be—
particularly from pupils who have not otherwise shown much imaginative flair in their prose writing. Often, remedial pupils can produce poems of real merit because they have been released from the
need to spell or punctuate correctly and because the intensity of writing a poem also helps them write in an exciting and imaginative way.
Telling pupils not to worry about the technical aspects of their writing in the first instance is important. It makes writing a poem like

a new start for some pupils. Using plain unlined paper can also assist here: pupils can write as roughly as they like and make additions and alterations. The lack of lines in a way symbolizes the new freedom.

Another approach is to write a class poem. Having chosen a subject—a tree in winter, the sea, a traffic scene or an animal—the class could be asked to contribute suitable descriptive words, phrases or comparisons to be written up on the board. Pupils can then be asked to write an eight or ten line poem about the subject using the material on the board if necessary.

Later on, simple two- or four-line rhyming stanzas can be used. Some of the poems of W. H. Auden can be effective models here (such as 'Roman Wall Blues' or 'O What is that Sound?' or 'Little Miss Gee'). An explanation of the rhyming scheme and the rhythm is necessary so that the pattern of the poem is clear before pupils are asked to go on to use the pattern for their own poems. Character sketches or simple stories in verse or parallel situations to the poems can be suggested. For instance, if 'Roman Wall Blues' is used as a model, pupils could be asked to imagine a different situation where a soldier writes home or someone on holiday writes about the bad weather and the inadequate hotel or an astronaut writes about the discomforts of being in space.

Here is one such version by a second year pupil:

A Sailor's Lament (on Columbus' World Voyage)

This smelly old ship is getting me down.
Oh to be back in my own native town,

Where the air is sweet and the weather is fine
And the grapes hang heavy on the vine.

Wine flows like water and maidens are fair.
My beautiful wife waits for me there.

My last voyage I'm sure this will be—
I'm terribly terribly sick of the sea.

Upon this ship we all are bound
To find out if the world is round.

And if it is and we get home,
This sailor never more shall roam.

DAVID WESTALL

After a few examples of free verse and simple stanza forms pupils can be left to choose their own medium when given the opportunity of writing a poem. In the course of time, after a few lessons throughout a year or so in which all pupils are expected to write poems, it is reasonable to give pupils a choice of writing in prose or verse. To go on insisting for too long that all pupils must write poems would be a mistake.

More light-hearted approaches to writing poetry can work as well. Comic forms such as limericks, clerihews, tongue-twisters, and other forms such as riddles, epitaphs, and the haiku are popular with young people. Again, a few models and some discussion of the required pattern can set pupils off writing their own examples.

Another possibility is to write a 'shape' poem where the pattern of the words on the page mirrors the subject. For instance, a poem about a snake would follow the undulating flow of a snake's body. Other suitable subjects for this kind of poem would be waves or fireworks or lightning.

A kind of poem which pupils find very approachable and which can result in imaginative work is the poem which consists of a list. It could be a list of similes or comparisons describing a person or an object. It could begin 'Her hair was as soft as silk', this first line setting the pattern and each following line consisting of a comparison. It could be a list of likes and dislikes; a list of things you might find on the seashore or in the countryside; a list of different things you associate with a particular colour; a list of pleasant or unpleasant sounds or tastes; a list of favourite or unfavourite foods. Another kind of 'list poem' is the 'definition poem' consisting of a series of definitions for loneliness or happiness or love or home.

Here are two examples of such poems:

I like the sound of sirens in police cars as they race to the scene of
   the crime.
I like the sound of records when they are put on at a speed faster
   than their usual.
I like the twang of an arrow as it leaves the bow.
I like the crackling of a fire as it burns viciously.
I like the sizzling of bacon and sausages.
I like the sound of church bells ringing on a Sunday morning.
I like the whizzing sound of racing cars as they race round the track.
I like the purring of a cat as she lies curled up on the mat in front
   of the fire.

I hate the repetitive drip of water as it drips in the empty sink.
I hate the crunching sound of ice when people bite it.

143

I hate the sound of interference on a radio when it is not tuned right.
I hate the squelching sound of water when it gets into your shoes.
I hate the gurgling sound that the sink makes as water runs down.
I hate the squeaky sound of rusty doors and gates that haven't been used for years.
I hate the thundering sound of pneumatic drills when used by workmen in the street.
I hate the sound of girls giggling when they're all gathered together.
I hate the bibbing of horns as they form a concerto in London traffic jams.
I hate the humming sound of the television when it is turned on too early in the morning.

MICHAEL HEMSLEY

Fear is getting mugged while walking home one night with your wages in your pocket.
Fear is meeting bully Briggs because you swore at him and are regretting it now.
Fear is travelling in an aeroplane.
Fear is when Russia launches a nuclear weapon aimed for America.
Fear is standing in high buildings and looking down below.
Fear is having a ride on a horse for the very first time.
Fear is watching Ali when he finally loses the world heavyweight title.
Fear is being caught by cops when in a hurry.
Fear is going to prison.
Fear is going to a new school and not knowing anyone.
Fear is being closed up in a small room.
Fear is watching a bull coming for you.
Fear is going to No. 7 to deliver a letter because of their dog.
Fear is going home alone.
Fear is being on duty at Manchester United ground.
Fear is when you think someone is watching you through a window.
Fear is being caught by cops when you are drunk.
Fear is travelling in a fast car.
Fear is being caught by guards while stealing diamonds from a jeweller's.
Fear is that your dad will beat you if you get a D or an E in English.
Fear is missing church one Sunday.
Fear is that your house will be burgled while you are out.

Fear is crossing a road.
Fear is you will drop off your skateboard and kill yourself.
Fear is buying your son one in the first place.

KURSHID FAIZ

Poems of this kind are in some ways synthetic, and no one is suggesting that the results would be high art. But they do provide a framework within which pupils can express their ideas. They provide an opportunity for discipline to be combined with imagination, and often the results reveal a higher standard than is achieved in other writing.

The poet Anthony Thwaite said that if he were locked in a room for an hour, he could produce a reasonable sonnet, but whether it would be a good poem or not would be another matter. In asking pupils to write poetry in the classroom, we are not expecting them to be poets or necessarily to produce good poems. There is something artificial and mechanical about the process. But the fact remains that the results can often be remarkable and creative.

A. Many examples of poems written by pupils are used in *New English*. For details, see the indexes of each volume. The following sections deal specifically with writing poetry:
NE1, Units 2 and 4;
NE2, Unit 4;
NE4, Unit 6.

B. For further advice on encouraging pupils to write poetry, see:
Explorations: A Practical Study of Children Writing Poetry, Rhodri Jones (McGraw Hill)
English Through Poetry Writing, Brian Powell (Heinemann)
Poetry Without Tears, Michael Baldwin (Routledge and Kegan Paul)
The Keen Edge, Jack Beckett (Blackie)
An Experiment in Education, Sybil Marshall (CUP)
Coming Into their Own, Marjorie L. Hourd and Gertrude E. Cooper (Heinemann)
For further examples of poems written by schoolchildren, see
Children as Poets, ed. Denys Thompson (Heinemann)
Children as Writers (Heinemann)
Enjoying Writing, ed. A. B. Clegg
The World in a Classroom, ed. Chris Searle (Writers and Readers Publishing Cooperative)

C. See also ADVANCED LEVEL, COMIC VERSE, CREATIVE WRITING, FIGURES OF SPEECH, MUSIC, PICTURES, POETRY.